Hansard Society

D0988480

The Hansard Society is the UK's leading independent, non-partisan political research and education charity. We aim to strengthen parliamentary democracy and encourage greater public involvement in politics.

President: Rt Hon Michael Martin MP, Speaker of the House of Commons.
Vice Presidents: Rt Hon Gordon Brown MP, Rt Hon David Cameron MP, Rt Hon Nick Clegg MP.

Hansard Society Scotland Parliamentary Patrons: Annabel Goldie MSP, Iain Gray MSP, Alex Salmond MSP, Tavish Scott MSP.

Hansard Society Scotland Working Group: Joyce McMillan (Chair), Jayne Ashley, Roy Cross, Michael Clancy OBE, Professor Charlie Jeffery, Dr Fiona Mackay, Roy Martin QC, Professor James Mitchell, Bill Thomson.

The Hansard Society has five main programmes of work: Hansard Society Scotland, Citizenship Education, Parliament and Government, eDemocracy and Study and Scholars. The Hansard Society also produces the well-established academic quarterly *Parliamentary Affairs* in association with Oxford University Press.

As a registered charity (in Scotland and in England & Wales), the Hansard Society relies on funding from individual donations, grants from charitable trusts and foundations, corporate sponsorship, and donations from individual parliamentarians from Holyrood, Cardiff, Belfast and Westminster. Our network of members and supporters come from all major political parties and from the public, private and third sectors. Those who support and work with us do so because we are independent and non-partisan, and our projects and programmes of work have genuinely made a difference to the democratic processes in the UK and beyond.

For further information visit our website at www.hansardsociety.org.uk

Recently, Hansard Society projects and activities have been funded and supported by:

Anglo American plc
BBC Parliament
BT
Bircham Dyson Bell LLP
Channel 4
ComRes

Corporation of London
DLA Piper
Department for Children, Schools and Families
E.ON UK
Educational Institute of Scotland
Electoral Commission
Ellwood & Atfield
European Parliament Office in Scotland
Foreign and Commonwealth Office
House of Commons
House of Lords
IBM UK Ltd
Joseph Rowntree Charitable Trust
Law Society of Scotland
Learning and Teaching Scotland
Lord Speaker
Luath Press
McGrigors LLP
Microsoft
Ministry of Justice
National Assembly for Wales
Nuffield Foundation
Open Society Foundation
PricewaterhouseCoopers LLP
Rio Tinto
Scotland Office
Scottish Enterprise
Scottish Parliament
Standard Life
UK Office of the European Parliament
Zurich Financial Services

The Scottish Parliament 1999–2009:

The First Decade

Edited by Charlie Jeffery and James Mitchell

Luath Press Ltd
EDINBURGH
www.luath.co.uk

HANSARD
SOCIETY

First published 2009 by Luath Press Ltd in association with

HANSARD
SOCIETY

Hansard Society Scotland
Thorn House, 5 Rose Street, Edinburgh EH2 2PR

Tel: 0131 243 2750. Email: hansard.scotland@hansard.lse.ac.uk

All rights reserved. No part of this publication may be reproduced, stored in a retrieval system or transmitted in any form by any means, without the prior permission of the Hansard Society.

The views expressed in this publication are those of the authors. The Hansard Society, as an independent, non-party organisation, is happy to invite analysis and discussion of these views.

For more information about other Hansard Society publications, visit www.hansardsociety.org.uk

Luath Press is an independently owned and managed book publishing company based in Scotland, and is not aligned with any political party or grouping. Luath has over 200 books in print including modern fiction, history, politics, travel guides, poetry and much more.

ISBN: 978-1-906817-21-3

Typeset by Luath Press

The paper used in this book is recyclable. It is made from low chlorine pulps produced in a low energy, low emissions manner from renewable forests.

Printed and bound by Bell & Bain Ltd., Glasgow

Text and graphics © Hansard Society 2009

Cover image © Scottish Parliamentary Corporate Body 2009

Contents

Foreword

For many of us, particularly for those who have been working in the Scottish Parliament since 1999, it is very hard to believe that 10 years have already passed by. It seems such a short time since that gloriously sunny day in July 1999 when the streets of Edinburgh were crowded with people to watch the newly elected MSPs process up the Royal Mile and into our temporary home on the Mound. But a decade it has been and, at this juncture, it is only right that we should pause to reflect on progress.

This particular publication will, I am sure, provide an interesting contribution to the many debates which will take place over the coming year about the impact of the Scottish Parliament. As a member of the parliament since 1999 and Presiding Officer since 2007, I have been privileged to see the institution grow and evolve from the inside. Although the parliament has not escaped controversy, and some criticism, over the last decade, I do believe it has achieved much: over 130 acts of parliament passed, numerous committee reports published, two million visitors and around 50,000 children through our education programme. Significant achievements in a short life.

During this time I believe we have also laid strong foundations on which the parliament can build. While our 10th anniversary is understandably about reflection, it must also be about looking forward to the type of institution we aspire to be in the future. As Presiding Officer, I hope that it will continue to strive to be an institution which serves all of Scotland's people.

I hope that you enjoy reading this publication and that many of you will also use this anniversary to engage – or re-engage – with *your* parliament.

Alex Fergusson MSP
Presiding Officer

Chapter 1

Introduction: The First Decade in Perspective

Emma Megaughin and Charlie Jeffery

High Expectations 1: Renewing Scottish Democracy

Rarely can such high expectations have been invested in a political institution as the Scottish Parliament. The words Winnie Ewing chose to open its inaugural session on 12 May 1999 were immensely significant: 'The Scottish Parliament, which adjourned on 25 March 1707, is hereby re-convened.' They were significant not just to those, like Ewing, who would prefer to see an independent Scotland, but also to the wider section of Scottish opinion that was comfortable with Scottish membership of the UK, but had become disillusioned with the way Scotland was governed within the UK. The experience of almost two decades of UK government, led by a Conservative Party with a Westminster majority, but able to win at best fewer than one third of the Westminster seats in Scotland, had called the legitimacy of the UK system of government into question in Scotland. Devolution – the establishment of a Scottish Parliament accountable to a Scottish electorate – was the response. The parliament was to democratise the government of Scotland, to make wide areas of decision-making much more directly accountable to the people those decisions affected.

High Expectations 2: A 'New Politics'

The expectations raised by the promise of democratic accountability were only one part of the story. The other had to do with the imagery attached by devolution campaigners in the 1980s and 1990s to the future parliament as an institution. The parliament was to become the fulcrum of a 'new politics'. That phrase has become tarnished and clichéd by its over-use. But it is worth looking back at what it signified. The new politics was defined both positively and negatively. Negatively it was about having a parliament, and a democratic process surrounding it, that was not like Westminster. Westminster was seen as too arcane, with too much antiquated pomp and ceremony, too remote and inaccessible and too much marked by an odd mix of clubbiness and a stylised adversarialism of opposition for its own sake. The new Scottish Parliament needed an institutional design and a way of working that would stand far removed from this negative example.

Much effort was put in the first half of the 1990s into working out more positively how the future Scottish Parliament would deliver a new politics. The Scottish Constitutional Convention brokered agreement between the Liberal Democrats and Labour on a form of proportional representation for the parliament that was designed to avoid the winner-takes-all logic of first-past-the-post and establish are operating a minority government and so whipping of all main parties has been stronger than usual. Party power has also increased as 'substitutes' are less likely to know committee business and so are more likely to follow the party line when they stand in for their absent party colleagues.

Compared with Westminster, another problem, which also reflects the smaller number of elected members available for committee service is that turnover of committee membership has been high, arguably preventing MSPs from acquiring detailed expertise in their fields. Within a year of the committee restructuring, the demise of First Minister McLeish in 2001 and his replacement by Jack McConnell contributed to a major rotation of the ministerial team, which had serious knock-on effects for the membership of the committees. The combination of committee restructuring and ministerial reshuffles in both 2001 and 2003 meant that the development of committee expertise was severely hampered in the early years, particularly for the opposition parties. There has been a similarly large-scale turnover of memberships following the change of government in 2007.

The Scrutiny Role
Compounding this matter even further is the breadth of remits of committees, particularly since 2007 when the number of committees was reduced from 19 to 14. Unlike Westminster, not only do many of the committees in Scotland have broader subject remits (for example, one committee covers economy, energy and tourism), but the subject committees combine the functions of both the Westminster standing committees and select committees as well as having additional powers to introduce legislation. Indeed, combination of functions in the Scottish Parliament means that resources and time are more stretched than they are at Westminster and this has arguably had most impact on the scrutiny function. If, for example, we compare the agenda of the Westminster transport committee with that of the Holyrood transport, infrastructure and climate change committee in March 2009, the Westminster transport committee held seven inquiries while the Holyrood transport committee only held one despite having a wider brief and remit. Of course, quantity says nothing about quality, or moreover, impact on government. However, impact will depend in part upon the number of reports, especially the capacity to return to a topic if it is not given adequate executive attention, and in this regard Westminster's two-tier committee system provides greater latitude for agenda setting and oversight of government. That said, Westminster oversight in some areas can also be ineffective, for example in the case of the Iraq war.

Another issue for the operation of committees is the rotation of governments. Opposition scrutiny using committees has arguably decreased since the election of a minority SNP Government. One of the reasons for this is that Labour and the Liberal Democrats are reluctant to engage in detailed scrutiny of policies that they had introduced under the previous administration. Instead, the current opposition appears to prefer using the debating chamber over the committees as the main forum for scrutiny. Since the debating chamber provides fewer avenues for detailed oversight, what we have now is arguably more theatre than scrutiny per se. Westminster general elections also have an impact on the work of committees, with reduced attendance and fewer committee reports in the month prior to a general election.

That said, committee scrutiny has not been without impact. Two parliamentary committee reports on the 2001 exams crisis prompted a no-confidence motion against the then children and education minister, Sam Galbraith. Other casualties of committee investigations include Labour leader Wendy Alexander who resigned in 2008 following pressures originating from the standards, procedures and public appointments committee. The committees have also challenged the executive over legislation that has contained insufficient substance for the committee to be able to pass judgment, for example the Primary Medical Services Bill in 2003. Subsequent procedures committee recommendations aimed at improving bill scrutiny were also approved in 2004, including more time for stage one inquiries, more time between stage one and stage two, and extra notice of amendments at both stages two and three.

Legislative Roles

A powerful legislative role for the committees was one of the key priorities of the CSG. It has been difficult to realise the CSG's ambitions. Opposition parliamentarians are disadvantaged in influencing Scottish government legislation because they: a) receive little or no support from the government in drafting amendments; b) and until 2007 government has invariably had the upper hand in terms of holding the majority of convener posts, and of having majority memberships on committees. There is at best limited evidence to suggest that parliamentarians in Scotland were more likely to be successful with their amendments than parliamentarians in Westminster. Moreover, parliamentarians on the government's side are more likely to succeed with their amendments; this may connect in part with controversies over the issue of (pre-2007) Scottish government provision of assistance to own-side MSPs in the wording of amendments.

That said, there is some evidence a small minority of substantive amendments passed in the executive's name were actually inspired by non-executive MSPs. But inter-party bargaining in committee is often very limited, and when it does happen it tends to be on very technical matters. Indeed, a procedures committee report on the operation of the founding principles warned that the parliament should not fall into the trap of becoming a 'conveyor belt for passing legislation'. There is a trade off: as committees become focused on government legislative business their capacity to scrutinise government through inquiries has reduced considerably over time.

cross-party cooperation and power-sharing, rather than adversarialism, as the modus operandi of Scottish politics. The Convention was also strongly influenced by a Scottish women's coordination group, which mobilised very effectively to ensure gender equality was an issue mainstreamed into the design of the parliament. In addition there was broader commitment to see the parliament work openly with 'civil society' which drew (rather haphazardly, it has to be said) on ideas of deliberative democracy and would open up the new Scottish democracy to participation by others than the 'usual suspects' in powerful interest groups. These equality and participation agendas would act as barriers against the kind of closed and clubby style of politics that Westminster represented.

All this was to be hard-wired into the design of the parliament. The Convention's final report in 1995 'expected' that the parliament would 'provide, through its practices and procedures a form of government in whose accountability, accessibility, openness and responsiveness the people of Scotland will have confidence and pride'. Bernard Crick and David Millar were commissioned by an Edinburgh think tank, the John Wheatley Centre, to prepare draft standing orders for the future parliament. Their report reinforced the sense of expectation attached to the parliament, not least in its title *To Make the Parliament of Scotland a Model for Democracy*. The report was marked by an overt 'not-like-Westminster' tone. There was a need 'to invent and adapt procedures and working practices better suited to an arising from Scotland's more democratic civic tradition', including a more consensual style of decision-making, greater accountability of the future Scottish government[1] to its parliament, in particular through a powerful committee system, and a much greater openness to public participation.

There is a clear lineage between the aspirations that Crick and Millar fleshed out and the report of the Consultative Steering Group (CSG) that was established in late 1997 to produce a blueprint on how the parliament should operate. As with the Convention and Crick/Millar, the language the CSG used was idealistic and rather high-blown. In his foreword the CSG chair, Henry McLeish, wrote, for example, of putting 'in place a new sort of democracy in Scotland'. This ideal was to be pursued through four key principles:

1.   The Scottish Parliament should embody and reflect the sharing of power between the people of Scotland, the legislators and the Scottish executive
2.   The Scottish executive should be accountable to the Scottish Parliament and the parliament and executive should be accountable to the people of Scotland

---

[1] The term 'government' is not entirely straightforward as a description of the Scottish government. In law it is formally the 'Scottish Executive'. The Labour First Minister Henry McLeish tried to adopt the terminology of 'Scottish Government' in 2001 but was slapped down by a UK government keen to reserve the term to itself. The SNP government elected in 2007 ignored UK government objections and simply rebranded itself as 'the Scottish Government', and the terminology is now generally used, except in Whitehall. Oddly enough, the adoption by the Welsh Labour First Minister Rhodri Morgan of the term 'Welsh Assembly Government' to describe his government was uncontroversial in Whitehall. As the Scottish government is by any comparative standards indeed 'a government', we use the term throughout.

3.	The Scottish Parliament should be accessible, open, responsive, and develop procedures which make possible a participative approach to the development, consideration and scrutiny of policy and legislation
4.	The Scottish Parliament in its operation and its appointments should recognise the need to promote equal opportunities for all

Expectations in Perspective

These were high ambitions. Much of this book is focused on answering how fully they have been met. The report card it draws up is mixed. The first years of the parliament were mired in controversy, in particular about the spiralling costs of the parliament building, but also a succession of scandals (as detailed by Brian McNair in Chapter 16). One consequence was a very sharp dip in public assessments of the parliament and its impact (see David McCrone in Chapter 13). This dip may not all have been to do with the parliament building and politicians' scandals. As James Mitchell has noted elsewhere, the rhetoric of a new politics that accompanied the parliament largely had to do with political *process*, and was largely an elite concern based on an analytical critique of Westminster government. What the broader public may have wanted rather more than a Rolls Royce political process was improved *policy outputs*. Of course process and outputs may well be linked, but with a time lag. In the short term, the general public, as David McCrone shows, felt that the parliament was not making much difference when it came to health, education or the economy. The idealistic imagery of a 'new politics', if it was interpreted not just as better political process but also as a promise of better policy, may well have magnified the disillusionment the public felt in the early years. The imagery of a new politics may have raised expectations that new politics *processes* were simply unable to deliver.

But there is another reason why the high expectations of the new politics could not easily be met: they were based on a misunderstanding of how the political process works. The Convention and the CSG systematically under-estimated the importance and the logic of party competition. Political parties are central to the operation of the Scottish Parliament. Though not as 'whipped' as at Westminster, they generally maintain high degrees of party discipline. The vision of the Convention and the CSG that Scotland would develop a form of consensus politics across and between parties was unrealistic. In particular, it underestimated the adversarial logic of the relationship between the two main parties in Scotland, the SNP and Labour. These have a deep and often visceral rivalry. That rivalry is in part about what divides them – in particular the constitutional question of union versus independence – but is also about what they share: an otherwise generally similar programmatic positioning – and competition for votes – to the left of centre. That deeply embedded rivalry translated itself easily to the Scottish Parliament's structures, investing the new with a good dose of the old.

In addition, as James Johnston notes in Chapter 4, the CSG's commitment to newness did not extend to government-parliament relations, on which its recommendations were rather conventional. The CSG placed the parliament in a reactive position vis-à-vis the government – in plenary session, in committee, and as individual MSPs – and even adopted classic Westminster techniques of accountability, such as parliamentary questions. While parliamentary question time has not been quite as ritualistically adversarial as at Westminster, the CSG's stipulation that 'the time provided in plenary for parliamentary questions should not be used for political point scoring' was over-optimistic. It under-estimated the power of party allegiance and party discipline to produce a Scottish version of the UK's adversarial party politics. It is striking that it was only when electoral arithmetic produced minority government in 2007 did a more widespread practice of cross-party cooperation emerge, though even this has been disguised by the cheerfully combative style adopted (especially towards his Labour opponents) by SNP First Minister Alex Salmond.

None of this is meant to suggest that the parliament has somehow failed in what it was intended to achieve. In many respects – as most of the chapters in this book confirm – it has brought a new and distinctive form of politics to Scotland. But what we do want to suggest is that we should not evaluate the parliament against a flawed benchmark. Much of the story the Convention and the CSG created about the parliament was overly idealistic, even naïve, and, with its emphasis on process over outputs, did not chime with the broader Scottish public. The Convention-CSG vision was not one that could be easily transformed into practice. But there is a different benchmark, as expressed by Winnie Ewing 10 years ago. That benchmark was about restoring legitimacy and accountability to the government of Scotland. There is now a Scottish democratic process (however 'new' or 'old' its features might be), based on Scottish elections, and carried out through a parliament able to give due attention to, and assure the legitimacy of, legislation and government action in Scotland. And, as Michael Keating and Paul Cairney show in Chapter 5, there is a new and substantial Scottish 'statute book' produced in that way. There may be some debate about how far Scottish elections are used to make judgements about what the Scottish Parliament and the government drawn from it do (see Chapter 12 by John Curtice and Chapter 11 by James Mitchell and Robert Johns), but there can be little doubt that the Scots firmly approve of their parliament. Indeed, if anything, they would like to see it do more. In this sense – the renewal of Scottish democracy – the high expectations invested in the parliament have been very clearly met.

This Book
This book is an attempt to record the achievements, and the limits of the Scottish Parliament over its first decade. It draws together assessments by the lively community of academics who work on the Scottish Parliament, some of those who have shaped the parliament in practice, and journalists who have

observed its work. These assessments are organised into sections: on the parliament in practice, the CSG's founding principles, representative process, the external stakeholders that engage with the parliament, and views on the parliament from other parts of the UK. A final chapter discusses how the Scottish Parliament fits in the UK's changing constitutional architecture.

Across the 21 chapters there is, as one would expect, no single assessment, but there are a number of themes that reappear. One is the contrast with practice at Westminster. There is perhaps something slightly obsessive and defensive about using Westminster as a (negative) benchmark. Some of the contributions – Richard Parry on quangos (Chapter 18), James Johnston on legislative process (Chapter 4) – hint that this might be a blind spot: in some areas the great Satan of Westminster might actually have better practice than the Scottish Parliament. The question this raises is when the Scottish Parliament might develop the self-confidence to learn from Westminster, rather than try to give it lessons.

A second theme is whether any aspiration to a new politics is ever going to prosper in an era of cynicism. James Mitchell once noted that devolution appeared not just to have repatriated Scottish politics, but also contempt for politics, politicians and parliament. There are echoes of his assessment here: in Joyce McMillan's discussion of the parliament against the background of a wider 'crisis of democracy' (Chapter 9); and Brian McNair's dispassionate analysis of why the media in Scotland routinely look beyond the everyday work of the parliament – most of it worthy and much of it effective – to focus on the negatives of scandals, expenses and cost overruns (Chapter 16).

A third theme is perhaps a little counter-intuitive: how little has changed in the substance of what the parliament does since the SNP came into government. Some of this has to do with minority arithmetic, but not all of it. Some has to do with sets of assumptions, shared across parties in Scotland, about doing politics in certain ways. So the opposition parties have not sought to become initiators of legislation in any significant way since 2007, though they could, because they share with the SNP the assumption that governments, not parliaments, should propose legislation. Some high profile policy issues aside, the direction of policy has not much changed since 2007, and nor have the relationships between government, parliament and outside stakeholders in local government, interest groups and quangos. Lindsay Paterson provides an explanation which some will find reassuring and others frustrating: that there is an elite-level consensus (and a congruence of social background) among MSPs, civil servants and the main professional interests outside parliament which has seamlessly made the transition from pre-1999 devolved administration to post-1999 democratic devolution (Chapter 15). If Paterson is right, the politics are not very new here either.

A fourth theme concerns the relationships of Scots and Scotland to the wider UK. Our chapters on representative process point – amid various contradictions and conundrums – to a political community of Scots beginning to define the boundaries of *their* democracy and its relationships to the wider UK democracy in which they are also members. Other chapters reverse the perspective, with Peter Riddell confirming what will not be a surprise to many: that post-devolution Scotland generally sits very low on London's radar (Chapter 19). Alan Trench by contrast suggests it is high on the Welsh radar – but not (as is often assumed) as a model the Welsh should emulate, but as an example of how the UK constitution has been able to flex to accommodate its component nations (Chapter 20). Charlie Jeffery takes that point further in discussing what he calls the UK's 'haphazard union' (Chapter 21).

A final theme is about the new political process to which the Convention and CSG aspired. The imagery of the new may have been overdone, but that does not mean that no progress has been made in realising some of the optimism and idealism that accompanied the establishment of the Scottish Parliament. Our chapters on the 'Parliament in practice' and the CSG's founding principles may present a mixed scorecard, but the mix includes real positives: in opening up the parliament to citizens and interest groups (not just Paterson's 'usual suspects'), in taking equal opportunities more seriously, in moving some way to using the parliament's committees to realise the founding principles, and in holding government to account. Minority government has also brought with it something closer to the power-sharing between parties that the Convention and CSG wanted to see.

We have no doubt that readers will see other themes and will disagree with our reading of the contributions we have assembled. The aim of the book is to prompt debate, not to provide a definitive view. That aim reflects where the idea for it came from: the Hansard Society Scotland Working Group, which was established in 2000 to accompany the new parliament. This book features many of those who have been members of the working group over the past nine years and many more who have supported the work of the Society.

Sir Bernard Crick 1929–2008

Sir Bernard Crick, who died in December 2008, wrote passionately for decades about the need for citizens to engage actively in politics, and to have education in how to do so, working through the Hansard Society to pursue that passion. He saw in the Scottish Parliament an opportunity to shape a political institution to support active engagement and what he called political literacy. He took that opportunity through his work with David Millar, which impacted directly on the CSG's recommendations. While he no doubt shared some of the disappointments set out in this book, he will have applauded those areas where the parliament has made a difference. This book is dedicated to his memory.

Chapter 2

A Dozen Differences of Devolution

Lord Steel of Aikwood

It is difficult to recall the true state of Scottish politics and public life before 1999. A major achievement of the Scottish Parliament is the bringing of the whole process of governance closer to the people. We can see that not only in the numbers of individuals and organisations who have come and given formal evidence to the committees, and in the number of petitions received and dealt with, but in the surprisingly heavy occupation of the public galleries, the amount of coverage on radio and television, and indeed the acreage of coverage – not all of course favourable – in our newspapers. Contrast all that with the distant operation of Scottish political life only 10 years ago. I am therefore cheered by opinion surveys which show that if the referendum were re-run fewer people than in 1997 would vote against devolution. It is here to stay.

The second achievement has been in the scale and scope of legislation. As Malcolm Rifkind memorably put it in the days of his enlightenment, Scotland had the only legal system in the world without a legislature to amend, adapt and improve it. The result was a log jam of reform waiting hopelessly in the Westminster timetable queue. Major reforms on topics such as mental health and land tenure, as well as committee and private members' bills, many of which were the subject of past unimplemented reports, were passed in the early days of devolution. It is my hope that future parliaments, having caught up the backlog, will spend less time legislating and more examining and scrutinising the government of the people.

This chapter provides me with an opportunity to list some of the differences between the Holyrood and Westminster parliaments, some or all of which might be regarded as improvements possibly to be followed by Westminster.

First, Holyrood has a fixed term of four years. The next election date does not have to be blamed on nor mulled over by any minister. This is a great convenience both for the political parties and for the public at large who can plan their own events accordingly. It also means that governments cannot hold the threat of an election over the heads of opposition parties – it takes a two-thirds majority to dissolve parliament inside the four year fixed term.

Second, Holyrood does not have annual 'sessions'. Bills do not fall at a certain date in the calendar as they do at Westminster. They can continue seamlessly through any of the four-year period.

Third, Holyrood is elected by proportional representation, which means a multi-party system with four main parties able to win constituency and list seats plus a number of smaller parties and independents mainly elected through the lists. It is difficult for one of those parties to obtain a 50% vote share and an outright majority. I would argue that this makes for more responsive and accountable government. In the Commons we have had governments with as low as 35% of the popular electorate support yet with a majority of MPs. The system in Scotland will frequently give rise to coalitions or minority government in which the government must take account of the views of parliament.

Fourth, Holyrood has a different shape. The U-shape of our chamber does not eliminate argument but it is designed to promote consensus, whereas at Westminster the parties are set in adversarial mode, two swords' lengths apart on the carpet.

Fifth, the Scottish Parliament keeps civilised hours, rarely sitting beyond six in the evening – our latest was, I think, 7.30pm. No stressed all night sittings.

Sixth, this family-friendly approach may well account for what I have just said. We have a much higher percentage of women in the Scottish Parliament than had hitherto been returned from Scotland at Westminster elections and amongst the highest in the world.

Seventh, the legislative procedure involves scrutiny before bills are debated in the chamber. Each bill is referred to the relevant subject committee for examination and discussion. People affected by the proposed legislation can come and give evidence to the committee which then delivers a report to the parliament as a whole. Thus our unicameral system, I believe, works just as effectively as the Westminster bicameral one in scrutinising and revising legislation. Indeed, I could argue that it works better by opening up the process more to the public.

Eighth, our petition system certainly opens up the process more to the public. At Westminster an MP can present a petition of signatures in a few sentences. It then goes into a bag behind the Speaker's chair and the signatures are counted. That is the last that is heard of it. In our parliament any one individual can petition the parliament on anything within its responsibilities. We have a petitions committee which receives these petitions and can either refer them to the appropriate minister or authority for answer, or to a committee of the parliament or, indeed, invite the petitioner to come and speak to their petition. In other words, action of some kind follows.

Ninth, at Westminster each session begins with the same Anglican prayer before proceedings are open to the public. We instead have a weekly slot called 'time for reflection' led each time in public session by members of the different faith communities in Scotland, roughly in turn according to the proportion of their adherents in Scotland – what we call proportional prayers! Again, I think this gives us a more positive outreach into society.

Tenth, Westminster did not use to webcast its proceedings. The House of Commons broadcasting committee's report in June 2000 commented, with admiration, on the Scottish Parliament's pioneering webcasting service. The service allows us to communicate not just with the Scottish electorate but all over the world. It is a free service, but we have registered users in Canada, Sweden, Japan, Thailand, New Zealand, Egypt, and of course England – to name but a few countries. All our registered users receive regular email updates on parliamentary business. There is great international interest in what we are doing with this 'cutting edge' broadcast medium. Holyrood has been specifically praised by the European Union for turning a good idea into a reality and advised the Queensland State Assembly in Australia on how they can best set up a similar service.

Our multi-channel service, which also includes committee coverage, I believe is the best parliamentary webcasting service in the world. We are certainly the only parliament broadcasting its proceedings over the web on broadband, near TV-quality pictures live onto computer screens.

Eleventh, as an open and inclusive parliament, its founders were clear from the outset that these principles must be extended to all – and that includes children and young people. To date, the Scottish Parliament has welcomed more than 54,000 school pupils and further education students as part of its inward education programme. More than 1.8 million people have visited the Scottish Parliament since 1999. Key to this is the emphasis on education – we have worked hard to demystify our procedures, and engender a genuine interest in the parliament as a working, accessible and relevant institution. Both the Westminster and Welsh Assembly education services have been greatly impressed by this approach and ethos – to the extent that they have revised their services to include, for example, a visits programme for younger children. The chamber itself has been the arena in which schoolchildren from across Scotland have met to debate issues such as young people's health, using the electronic voting system, and having their contributions broadcast around the world via the internet. This tangible demonstration of genuine accessibility would, I believe, be unattainable at Westminster.

Twelfth, a new parliamentary building at Holyrood has been created. Like Portcullis House, the proposed Holyrood building has attracted many column inches in the newspapers about the cost of the building. The difference, of course, is that we in Scotland are getting a national parliament complete with a debating chamber, members' accommodation, committee rooms and staff accommodation.

Portcullis House is essentially a building where less than half of the MP have their offices. In 1894, *The Times* reported that the cost of the new Houses of Parliament at Westminster was exceeding the original estimate by 350%, and urged 'the greatest economy by postponing portions of the building and even the sacrifice of decorative style etc'. Most of us are thankful that our Victorian forefathers completed the Palace of Westminster, including Big Ben, without such sacrifice and I am confident that future generations of Scots will be equally grateful for Enric Miralles's design at Holyrood.

Challenges

I want to make an observation about parliaments generally and one specifically about both Holyrood and Westminster. Politics is becoming a dangerously closed shop in all parties. When I first entered the Commons, it was full of people with different experiences of life, having worked as miners or steel-workers, bankers, owners of landed estates. We even had a rear-admiral. Now the most common route to a seat in either parliament is to have been a party researcher, local official or councillor. It is a chicken and egg question. When I hear officials of business organisations complain about the lack of experienced business people in parliament I am tempted to ask how many in their organisation bother to take part in or even join a political party. The remedy lies in the hands of the electorate.

Second, we could do with some 'revising' mechanism for legislation. I have mentioned this in passing before and been caricatured for my pains as proposing to establish a Scottish House of Lords, which I emphatically do not. Some have argued that our unicameral parliament is flawed and that it ought to be bicameral to provide a check and balance as the House of Lords does at Westminster. I have never agreed with that proposition, and I do not detect a thirst among the population for yet more politicians and elections. But I do recognise that the total absence of any check could present problems.

One of the merits of the Scottish procedure is that we timetable all bills by agreement, compared to my time in the House of Commons when guillotines were regularly imposed on the later stages of bills and quite often amendments were voted on without time for any debate on them. The Commons have, since 2000, voted on programme motions and for timetabling bills, though amendments still go undebated. That is not too serious because they are usually picked up in the House of Lords. Their general power to ask the elected House to think again is, if sparingly and sensitively used, also useful. The Scottish Parliament has no such mechanism. I can tell you that there were a couple of occasions when I had doubts about the tightness of a bill's timetable and I made it clear that I regarded it as wholly unacceptable that we should vote on any amendments to legislation without discussion. I decided that if that were about to happen I would suspend the sitting and seek the introduction of a fresh timetable. Fortunately I never had to carry out my threat, though we came within seconds of it on a couple of occasions.

There is already one limited failsafe check. After a bill is passed by the parliament we have to wait for a month while the UK law officers certify that it has not fallen foul of either the Scotland Act or the European Convention on Human Rights. Only then does the Presiding Officer write to the Queen asking her to give her royal assent, at which point it becomes an act and passes into the law of the land. All I am suggesting is that, during that same month, bills could be referred to an appointed committee of a couple of dozen people.

Their task should be to pick up any perceived defects or widespread objections. They should have the capacity neither to oppose nor alter what the elected parliament has done, but merely to refer a bill or part of it back for a further examination by the parliament.

They could meet in one of the of the committee rooms at minimal public expense. Whether they are called the revising committee or constitute a revival of the Scottish Privy Council, abolished at the time of the Union, is unimportant. They should be men and women independent of the political parties (though some could perhaps be suggested by them) and represent a broad spectrum of Scottish civic life, perhaps replacing the now rather aimless Civic Forum. The Prime Minister's Appointments Commission could make the necessary selection.

Conclusion
The Scottish Parliament has already influenced the Westminster one. During his time as leader of the Commons Robin Cook visited us twice and Gareth Williams as leader of the Lords once. Both chambers operate more family-friendly hours than they used to; they have started pre-legislative scrutiny; expanded their educational outreach; and 'carry over' bills have been introduced which do not fall at the end of the session. I accept that imitation is the sincerest form of flattery.

Chapter 3

Committees in the Scottish Parliament

Chris Carman and Mark Shephard

During the deliberations of the Constitutional Convention and the Consultative Steering Group great concern was expressed as to how the future Scottish Parliament would most appropriately check the power of the Scottish government. The solution was to use 'strong' committees to rein in the government when necessary. In order to achieve this, all-purpose parliamentary committees were established with powers to initiate, scrutinise and investigate legislation, and to be capable of playing a central role from an early stage in the legislative process. In these legislative roles the committees are broadly comparable to Westminster standing committees. But they also took on scrutiny roles similar to those of Westminster select committees, with powers to conduct inquiries and take evidence from ministers and civil servants.

Two different types of committees are used in the Scottish Parliament to carry out the roles of scrutinising the government as well as ensuring that the parliament is a full participant in the law-making process. Mandatory committees are established under the parliament's standing orders with defined remits and include: standards, procedures and public appointments; public petitions; and equal opportunities. In addition, subject committees are established at the beginning of each parliamentary session and are designed broadly to reflect the briefs of the Scottish government's ministers, for example: economy, energy and tourism; health and sport; and justice.

In his classic analysis of committees in European parliaments Kaare Strom noted that committee powers can be divided into several categories: (1) the committees' right to initiate legislation, (2) the right to rewrite bills, (3) their control of the committees' timetable and (4) their methods of obtaining information[1]. The more of these 'rights' the committees have, the more powerful they are in the parliament concerned. In the Scottish Parliament, committees have the right to initiate legislation (1) and they can propose amendments to bills (2). They have less control of the timetable (3) as committee work has tended to be driven by the priorities and time constraints of the government, from whom information (4) has not always been forthcoming. Of course, information can be sought from outside of government, and there have been some successes on this front, most noticeably in the openness and participation that the committees have worked hard to foster.

[1] K. Strom (1998), 'Parliamentary Committees in European Democracies', in L.D. Longley and R.H. Davidson, eds. *The New Roles of Parliamentary Committees* (London: Frank Cass).

Strom also notes that the later a committee enters the process, the less influence it has in the chamber. Compared with Westminster, committees in the Scottish Parliament invariably enter into the legislative process at an earlier stage. They consider a proposal's general principles during stage one of a bill's consideration and pass their view (positive or negative) to the whole chamber. Provided there is parliamentary acceptance (based on the committee's report) of the bill's principles, the bill will be referred back to the lead committee for detailed 'line-by-line' consideration. It is at this stage that the committee will consider amending the bill. During the first and second stages, committees may take evidence and request information from ministers (it is expected that ministers will respond either in person or in writing). Finally, the amended bill, if passed out of the committee, is then referred to the whole chamber. At this third stage the chamber may pass the bill or refer it back to the committee for further 'stage two' consideration.

Before evaluating the committees according to the above criteria, and in comparison with Westminster, it is important to bear in mind the four driving principles that the Consultative Steering Group (CSG) highlighted, which are often used as benchmarks with which to assess the work of the parliament. The four principles are: accountability; power-sharing; access and participation; and equal opportunities.

In terms of accountability and power-sharing, the CSG envisaged that the committees would initiate legislation, scrutinise and amend the Scottish executive's proposals, and have wide-ranging investigative functions. To distinguish between the procedural and political control over the committees, the CSG recommended committees adopt a 'reporter' system as is often used in European parliaments. To increase public access and participation to the parliament, the committees were encouraged to meet throughout Scotland, perhaps even permanently basing some of the committees outside Edinburgh. Committees would also help to encourage participation through the public petitions system and open consultations with Scottish civic society. Additionally, the committees were urged to institute continuing expert panels to inform their decisions. It was also envisaged that committee meetings should be open to members of the public (as would most meetings of the parliament).

Finally, it was envisaged that the parliament would establish an equal opportunities committee to both promote equality throughout Scotland as well as monitor the activities of the government to ensure that they conformed with the broad goal of promoting an inclusive Scotland.

Constraints on the Committees
During the first year of the Scottish Parliament it became apparent that MSPs and committee staff faced serious time and resource pressures. Committee work proved to be more onerous than anticipated. Compared with Westminster,

committees at Holyrood not only tend to consider legislation earlier in the legislative process (see above), but they also combine law-making with scrutiny roles. There are also fewer elected representatives to serve on committees, implying a higher average workload: compared with the House of Commons, the Scottish Parliament has over five times fewer politicians (129 MSPs compared with 646 MPs). One solution to this inbuilt overload was to reduce the numbers of members serving on committees. The aim was to allow MSPs more time to devote to their committee work by reducing the number of committee responsibilities they had, and to give committee staff more time to devote to fewer voices.

In December 2000, the parliamentary bureau successfully moved a resolution to reorganise the committee system and in January 2001 committees were restructured and renamed. Key to this was the quite radical reduction in numbers per committee (typically from 11 to seven MSPs per committee). In the first year (1999-2000) of the Scottish Parliament, a total of 103 MSPs sat on one or more committees: 43 on one; 54 on two; and six on three. By the 10th year (2008-09) 87 MSPs sat on one or more committees: 65 on one; 22 on two; and zero on three. In another step to manage workloads more flexibly, the Scottish Parliament decided to permit the nomination of 'substitute' committee members with voting rights who could stand in for absent colleagues. In addition, to reflect volume of legislation by policy domain, committee names and briefs have been altered throughout the first 10 years, for example, following the 2001 reorganisation, two justice committees were created from one former committee, though have since been re-combined.

There are a number of consequences of the reformed committee system, both positive and negative. On the upside, MSPs have had more time to devote to committee work, and been better supported to do so. On the downside, the changes altered the power balance away from MSPs and towards parties, as having fewer slots per committee increased the competition for places, making support of the party line more important in both selection and maintenance of committee posts. Indeed, several MSPs appear to have been removed from committees for challenging the party line, for example, in 2003, Labour's Karen Gillon was quite critical of the (then) executive for its response to committee investigations of school closures, which came hot on the heels of committee disquiet over assessment practices. At the next meeting of the education committee she was no longer convener. Parliamentarians do not have to do what their parties want, for example, Dorothy Grace-Elder refused to leave the health and community care committee in 2002. However, the consequences are invariably severe as her party (SNP) voted to suspend her from the party and she departed the parliament at the next election. Party leaders have on occasion levelled threats at MSPs that they could be punished for not following the party line by removal from their 'chosen committee'. Pressure on MSPs to toe the line has arguably increased since 2007 as the SNP

One of the main differences between Westminster and Holyrood is that committees in the Scottish Parliament can initiate committee bills. The first committee bill was introduced in 2001 and in the first session three committee bills passed, dropping to one in session two, and one so far in session three. One of the difficulties for committees is finding time and cross-party consensus to be pro-active in introducing committee bills legislation. Arguably the most important hurdle to committee success has been the power of the parliamentary bureau (PB) to set agendas. The PB has tended to give priority to the government's legislative agenda. Indeed, the bulk of committee time is reactive to government legislation and actions. That said, compared with Westminster, committee and parliamentary support for members' bills is arguably better and this can mean that members can use committees to set agendas. For example, a member's bill on prohibiting smoking in public places played a significant contribution in driving the McConnell government's commitment to a smoking ban in indoor public places. In quantitative terms though, the proportion of non-executive legislation passed from 1999-2007 was just over 12%, which was almost identical to that at Westminster. If anything, the figure is likely to fall over time as rules on introducing members' bills were tightened in 2004, adding: consultation periods; increased signature requirements; limits on bills per MSP; and providing the executive with rights to intervene where it or the UK is envisaging taking action.

Finally, while committees might at times prompt the passage of legislation, if the financial resources are not in place to implement it, then a tally of bills passed is not necessarily a measure of success. In the case of the Homelessness Act (2003), for example, targets for eliminating homelessness are unlikely to be met due to a number of problems including funding issues and the availability of affordable housing. This example also raises the issue of post-legislative scrutiny, which given the already crowded agendas faced by the committees is very rare in Scotland.

At the outset, the parliament worked hard to deliver on openness and participation. During the first session, committees had held 51 full formal meetings outside Edinburgh. However, the number of committee meetings held outside Edinburgh declined over the next session to 41 meetings, and based on current figures, looks set to decline even more in session three. Delivering openness and participation requires significant resources as well as the commitment and drive of the MSPs and indeed the clerks of the committees themselves. By the end of the first session of the parliament, parliamentarians increasingly found that encouraging public participation has severe knock-on effects on workloads. Committee conveners complained that the large number of petitions forwarded for committee consideration consumed a significant amount of time and staff energy. One consequence was a dramatic cut in the number of petitions referred to committees in the second session, with the public petitions committee closing a far greater percentage of petitions after initial consideration. Arguably of more success has been the principle of equal opportunities. The parliament established a mandatory equal opportunities committee and its presence has provided institutional legitimation and *raison d'être* for assisting in easing through less than populist proposals such as abolition of Section 28A (limiting education on homosexuality in schools), as well as for raising the profile through inquiries of disadvantaged groups, most notably the disabled.

Conclusion

Perhaps the CSG principles are best considered as ideals to work towards. What Scotland has now is clearly far better at delivering the CSG principles than what existed pre-devolution. But there are still clear limits which the CSG perhaps underestimated. In particular, party is key in Scotland, just as it is in Westminster, and any hopes of doing business radically differently have been hampered ultimately by party control of: the legislative agenda; committee membership; and committee operation. Any hopes that the committees would be the vehicles of a 'new politics' have arguably been dashed as a closer analogy is that committees have primarily become the engine rooms for the passage of majority-backed legislation from 1999 to 2007, or intensely partisan political squabbles and little actual legislation since 2007.

Chapter 4

The Legislative Process: The Parliament in Practice

James Johnston

Introduction
In setting out its proposals for the legislative process, the Consultative Steering Group (CSG) stated that 'we have been influenced in particular by our key principles of power-sharing and access and participation'. In this chapter, I will suggest that the Scottish Parliament has been bold and innovative in facilitating access and participation within the legislative process. In terms of sharing power, however, the CSG's commitment to a traditional view of executive-legislature relations made a radical restructuring of the law-making process much less likely.

By far the most significant aspect of the parliament's legislative procedures is the role of the parliamentary committees. In a unicameral system, it is the committees which take on the role performed elsewhere by revising chambers like the House of Lords at Westminster. Over the first 10 years, the committees have approached this role with a real verve and enthusiasm, firmly establishing themselves as the engine room of the parliament. However, in no meaningful sense can the committee system be viewed as power-sharing with the Scottish government. Rather, the emphasis has been on ensuring the effective scrutiny of the government.

Access and Participation
The CSG emphasised access and participation as a 'cornerstone' of its recommendations. In particular, it argued that there should be a 'participative approach to the development, consideration and scrutiny of policy and legislation'. From the outset, therefore, the parliament sought to facilitate a participative approach to its legislative scrutiny. In particular, there has been a desire to engage with those most likely to be affected by proposed legislation. This has led to a concern not only to make the process transparent and accessible, but also to be proactive in seeking to reach out to those groups and individuals who would not normally engage with the political process.

This emphasis on public engagement has resulted in much more detailed scrutiny of proposals at the pre-legislative stage and stage one of the legislative process than was anticipated by the CSG. Although the scrutiny role at this stage is ostensibly to look at the 'general principles', the committees have tended to look much more closely at bills, including suggesting amendments to the executive. This has allowed for much greater public involvement in the legislative process than exists at Westminster.

Mindful of the need to engage widely, the committees have also been keen to adopt an innovative approach to obtaining evidence at the pre-legislative stage and at stage one. These have included:

- Round-table discussion forums at committee meetings
- Committee meetings outside Edinburgh
- Fact-finding visits at a pre-legislative stage
- Providing an opportunity for contributions from the public at meetings
- Conferences in the chamber

In its legacy paper at the end of the 2003–07 session of the parliament, the environment and rural development committee reflected on the three committee meetings outside Edinburgh it held as part of its stage one inquiry on the Crofting Reform etc. bill. The committee noted that it 'considers that the opportunities this allowed for hearing very directly from people affected by the proposed legislation enabled it to scrutinise the bill more effectively'.

The communities committee, in preparing for the introduction of the Planning etc. Scotland bill, organised a conference in the chamber for members of the public and representatives of community groups, as well as a further three events for planning professionals, councillors and developers. The committee stated in its legacy paper that it 'found these four events very useful as it was well informed of the various viewpoints of key stakeholders before initiating the formal consideration of the legislation'.

The education committee noted in its legacy paper that it held a round-table evidence session involving stakeholders from the voluntary sector at stage one of the Protection of Vulnerable Groups (Scotland) bill. It held three events involving people whose lives had been affected by adoption to inform its stage one consideration of the Adoption and Children (Scotland) bill. The committee also held formal meetings in Skye and Glasgow during its scrutiny of the Gaelic Language (Scotland) bill.

Power-Sharing?

As demonstrated by this brief summary of committee engagement, the parliament's report card for its first 10 years is likely to contain pass marks for its achievements in relation to access and participation. But, as the previous Presiding Officer, George Reid, pointed out in his 2006 Stevenson lecture on citizenship, 'the fourth principle of the sharing of power between government, people and parliament remains elusive'. This is hardly surprising. The CSG was markedly more conservative in its approach to power-sharing than the other core principles, especially in its recognition that the legislative process would be primarily led by the executive: the government would introduce legislation and the parliament would ensure effective law-making. On this basis the legislative process is little different from Westminster.

The CSG proposed a hybrid model of 19th century representative government and 21st century participatory democracy. On the one hand, the aim was to create an 'open, accessible and above all, participative parliament', while on the other hand recognising 'the need for the executive to govern'. The emphasis on a more participative parliament was clearly limited by the CSG's expectation that the majority of legislation would originate from the executive. Furthermore, the CSG did not envision the parliament having a role in the policy development process. Again, this was viewed as the responsibility of the executive who would be expected to allow groups and individuals the opportunity to influence the development of policy, as opposed to being invited to comment on draft legislation. Parliament's role was to be restricted to monitoring the executive's consultative process.

Pre-Legislative Scrutiny

A prime example of the influence of the CSG's conservative proposals on power-sharing is the committees' approach to pre-legislative scrutiny. Rather than being seen as an opportunity to engage with the government on draft policy proposals, it has instead tended to be a precursor to the formal legislative process. As set out in the parliament's *Guidance on Public Bills*, this form of scrutiny 'can be useful in allowing members to familiarise themselves with the subject-matter prior to introduction'. Given that a committee is not due to report until the end of its stage one inquiry, it is unlikely that it would wish to pre-empt its findings by making recommendations to the executive based on any pre-legislative consideration. Pre-legislative scrutiny is, therefore, not viewed as a mechanism through which to seek changes to government legislation before it is introduced.

A 2004 report by the procedures committee, while recognising the potential benefits of pre-legislative scrutiny, identified a number of drawbacks. It suggested that committees may compromise their perceived independence as a detached and critical scrutineer if they seek to develop a role as a partner in the law-making process. The committee concluded that pre-legislative scrutiny should not be 'expected as a normal part of the legislative process'.

In contrast, at Westminster there have been recent moves towards a greater role for the parliament in seeking to influence legislation before it is introduced. In 1997, the first report of the newly established modernisation committee concluded that pre-legislative scrutiny:

> Provides an opportunity for the House as a whole, for individual back-benchers, and for the opposition to have a real input into the actual form of legislation which subsequently emerges, not least because ministers are likely to be far more receptive to suggestions for change before the bill is actually published.

The committee suggested that parliamentary scrutiny may be more effective before policy positions become firmly entrenched. It identified a number of draft bills – such as the Communications bill and the Civil Contingencies bill – where the government accepted a number of amendments before introducing the bills to parliament. Following a more recent inquiry, the committee concluded that 'the introduction of pre-legislative scrutiny is generally acknowledged to be one of the most successful innovations in the process in recent years'. The committee identified three main goals in carrying out pre-legislative scrutiny: public engagement; better law-making; and achieving consensus.

But while the modernisation committee argued for an increase in pre-legislative scrutiny at Westminster, the number of draft bills published by the UK government has remained relatively small and they are generally uncontroversial. There is also little opportunity for public engagement elsewhere in the legislative process, although in 2006 the standing committees that made detailed line-by-line consideration of bills were replaced by public bill committees which have the power to receive written and oral evidence from outside parliament.

Pressures on the Committee System
Given the willingness of Holyrood's committees to conduct wide-ranging consultations on proposed legislation, it was not long before concerns began to emerge in relation to the amount of legislation and the impact on effective scrutiny. The number of bills introduced rose from 73 in the first session (1999-2003) to 81 in the second session (2003–07). The number of executive bills also rose from 51 to 53. This led to some tension between the executive and the parliament, as reflected in the legacy papers of the Conveners Group (CG) in both the first and second sessions. In particular, the CG agreed that the high number of executive bills meant that some committees were essentially executive led, with little opportunity to pursue their own work programmes.

Following the concerns raised by the CG at the end of the first session, the procedures committee carried out an inquiry into the amount of time allowed for the consideration of public bills. The committee recognised that these concerns were being voiced, not only by backbenchers, but also by the executive. For example, in April 2003, *The Scotsman* published an interview with the then First Minister, Jack McConnell, in which he acknowledged that bad laws could result from the executive and parliament rushing to enact legislation. Following the procedures committee report, a number of procedural changes were agreed by the parliament aimed at increasing the minimum timescales between each of the legislative stages.

Despite these procedural changes, concerns continued to mount during the second session that many committees were increasingly overburdened with legislation. This can be seen in the fall in the number of committee inquiries from 166 in the first session to 99 in the second session, of which 11 were short inquiries. These concerns dominated the CG's legacy paper at the end of the second session, which stated that: 'The group has serious concerns about the number of bills introduced and referred to committees in the second session.' A number of difficulties were identified as being caused by the high level of legislation:

- Weekly and sometimes twice weekly meetings rather than fortnightly
- Insufficient time to adequately prepare for meetings
- An inability to undertake other scrutiny work including inquiries
- An inability to conduct post-legislative scrutiny

The CG expressed its concern that the potential impact of these constraints was that 'poor legislation will be enacted without proper detailed scrutiny' and that 'large and important areas of executive policy and administration do not receive the appropriate level of scrutiny by parliamentary committees'.

While the CG made a number of recommendations aimed at reducing the legislative burden on the committee system, these have been superseded by the arrival of minority government. Given the obvious difficulties which a minority government faces in securing a majority for its legislative programme within the parliament, there has been a substantial reduction in the amount of government legislation being introduced in session three. Somewhat surprisingly, however, this has not led to a marked increase in non-legislative scrutiny by those committees which had been over-burdened by legislation in the first two sessions.

Committee Bills

Arguably, the most radical aspect of the parliament's legislative procedures is the ability of committees to initiate legislation. It was envisioned by the Scottish Constitutional Convention that committee bills would be a regular feature within a parliament which was much less executive-led than Westminster. The committees' right of legislative initiative was, as David Arter noted, 'part of the general reaction against executive-dominant, party-dominant politics of Westminster'.[1] As such, committee bills were viewed at the outset of the parliament as a key means of sharing power.

That view has not turned into practice. From 1999–2007 just four committee bills were enacted. Given the pressures on the committee system identified above, and the substantial resources required to introduce legislation, this would seem a reasonable number. At the same time, this legislation has been limited in its scope: two of the bills related to internal parliamentary procedure and the other two were single issue bills.

---

[1] D. Arter (2004), 'The Scottish Committees and the Goal of a "New Politics": A Verdict on the First Four Years of the Devolved Scottish Parliament', *Journal of Contemporary European Studies*, 12, 1, p. 7.

In the third session, as the constraints on committees have lessened with the fall in the amount of legislation introduced by government, it may have been anticipated that some committees would have sought to exploit the current gaps in their own work programmes to bring forward their own legislation. This has not happened. Despite its minority status, the onus remains firmly on the government to bring forward its legislative programme.

Members' Bills

A further radical aspect of the legislative process is the innovative approach to members' bills. MSPs were keen from the outset that the process for members' bills at Holyrood was properly resourced. This would ensure that, unlike Westminster where little resources are made available within the House of Commons in support of private members' bills, such legislation would have a realistic chance of making it to the statute book in the Scottish Parliament. This led to the establishment of the non-executive bills unit (NEBU), which provides support for members and committees in developing and drafting proposed legislation. Unsurprisingly the demand for members' bills within the new parliament quickly led to the need to establish 'prioritisation criteria'. However, concerns over parliamentary officials being responsible for prioritising members' bills led to the matter being referred by the parliamentary bureau to the procedures committee at the beginning of the second session.

Having been unable to find a means of agreeing prioritisation criteria, the procedures committee instead recommended 'a substantially more rigorous and structured procedure' for the introduction of members' bills. This included increasing the threshold of support from 11 to 18 members; a requirement to carry out a consultation period of at least 12 weeks; and the need to have the support of members from at least half of the political parties or groups represented in the parliamentary bureau.

Although there was some opposition to the proposals, they were eventually passed unanimously by the parliament. The thrust of the procedural changes was that, while individual members should have the opportunity to initiate legislation, it is not appropriate to seek to achieve narrow party political goals through this process. Proposals should be well thought out and have broad appeal.

Conclusion

In drafting its proposals for the legislative process, the CSG broadly got it right. Whether deliberately or not, it anticipated that there would be agreement among the political parties that it is for the government to govern and, therefore, legislation should be primarily executive-led. Any proposals to dilute the government's power of legislative initiative, such as the procedures committee's idea for a 'task force' (involving opposition MSPs in policy development) have been criticised as blurring the lines of accountability.

Even with a minority government, it is still expected that the government will bring forward the bulk of legislation. So, even though the current SNP administration lacks the numbers to get its policies on the statute book, it still gets criticised – as by the Labour leader in the Scottish Parliament, Iain Gray, for its 'puny legislative programme'. But there has been no rush by the opposition to fill the legislative void. They remain comfortable with the Westminster model of law-making and an opportunity for a greater share of spoils come the next election. Yet, the legislative process does have a radical feel to it. While power-sharing remains elusive, the legislative process is both accessible and transparent allowing the more participative politics envisioned by the CSG.

Chapter 5

The New Scottish Statute Book: The Scottish Parliament's Legislative Record since 1999

Michael Keating and Paul Cairney

A distinctive feature of Scottish devolution compared with other countries is that Scotland has always had its own statute book, with distinct Scottish legislation over a range of policy fields. Some of this consisted of separate Scottish bills, but a lot of it took the form of Scottish clauses tacked onto UK bills, making the statute book somewhat untidy and not easy to follow. Most Scottish MPs tended to specialise in Scottish legislation, which was dealt with largely by the Scottish Grand Committee and Scottish standing committees, isolating it from the Westminster mainstream. While they jealously guarded their prerogatives in these matters, the policy content of legislation was not greatly different from that pursued in England and Wales, given government dominance of the process and the fact that the essential second reading and report votes were taken in the whole House. Standing committees were also nominated to ensure a government majority, with English MPs being drafted in during the later years of the Conservative government in order to make up the numbers.

One effect of devolution has been an increase in separate Scottish bills. From an average of six bills per year at Westminster between 1979 and 1999, the number increased to an average of 15 per year in the first session of the Scottish Parliament (1999-2003) and 17 in the second (2003-07). The first year of the third session saw only five bills passed, a not surprising outcome since the new SNP government lacked a parliamentary majority. A further effect of devolution has been to open up the possibility of a different legislative agenda and different policy content as compared with Westminster.

The First Session: 1999–2003
The first session's legislation showed strong continuity from pre-devolution days, as Labour ministers merely moved from the Scottish Office to the Scottish executive, albeit in coalition this time with the Liberal Democrats. Of the 61 bills passed (including 50 from the executive), 13 were essentially the same as legislation passed at the same time in Westminster, often cut and pasted so that the wording was identical. Some of these arose from international obligations, such as the international criminal court, while others were spillovers. For example, one law banned fur farms, even though there were none in Scotland, because fur-farmers could have moved there after the ban in England. Nine bills contained essentially the same policy as their Westminster counterparts, but with some scope for variation in application. Eight dealt with the same issue as

equivalent England and Wales legislation but applying a different policy. In some cases, the differences looked small but were potentially important, such as the wording of the Freedom of Information Act, which was rather more liberal in Scotland. Finally, 20 Holyrood bills had no counterpart at all at Westminster. These ranged from housekeeping matters for which time had not been found before, to historic items like the Land Reform Act, a measure demanded since the 19th century, as well as the Annual Budget Act.

Not all of these distinctive Holyrood bills represented a divergence from England. As well as changing the relationship between Scotland and the United Kingdom, devolution shifted power within Scotland, allowing measures that had previously been blocked by vested interests well connected to the old Scottish Office system or neglected for want of time. The abolition of feudal tenure was a complex and overdue measure needing concentrated attention. National Parks had been blocked in the 1940s by landowner pressure within Scotland, while proceeding in England and Wales. The abolition of poindings and warrant sales ended a Scottish practice widely regarded as out of place in modern society.

Relatively few pieces of legislation stood out as beacons of a different legislative agenda. Acts to introduce 'free personal care' for older people (or at least heavily subsidise personal care at home) and abolish up-front tuition fees and replace them with an endowment payment upon graduation represented the flagship policies of the first session and introduced potentially significant divergence from the rest of the UK. Two education acts reinforced existing policy differences based on a Scottish commitment to comprehensive education and local authority control of schools. The Mental Health Act 2003 accelerated differences established before devolution (including the significant absence in Scotland of controversial plans to preventatively detain people with personality disorders) and, perhaps more importantly, reinforced the idea of a 'Scottish policy style' involving relatively close and consensual relationships between government and interest groups, or policy-makers and those they consult.

The Second Session: 2003-07

These trends continued in the 2003-07 session. Sixty-seven bills were passed of which 53 were executive bills, but a systematic divergence of policy direction was never established. Instead, we can detect trends in policy priorities. Labour's Cathy Jamieson replaced the Liberal Democrat Jim Wallace as justice minister following Labour suggestions that the Liberal Democrats were 'soft on crime', and promoted an extensive series of bills (approximately one-quarter of all executive legislation) addressing the justice system, sentencing, weapon crime, prostitution and introducing anti-social behaviour orders (ASBOs) to deal with behaviour associated with certain sections of the population in what the press inevitably labelled the 'war on neds'. Most of the legislation was very much in line with the UK Labour government's increasing emphasis on being more 'tough on crime' than 'tough on the causes of crime', marking a reframing of policy from social exclusion and disadvantage to social misconduct. Yet, there was considerable scope for variation in application, since local authorities in Scotland proved reluctant to use ASBOs as a form of social control and (given Scotland's distinct judiciary) Scottish ministers were much less likely to be embroiled in the need for sentencing reforms following high-profile cases. Overall, if the first session displayed continuity, then the second demonstrated incrementalism, with most bills focused on reforming the details of existing provision on matters such as crofting, legal aid, bankruptcy, aquaculture, adoption, school meals, alcohol licensing, housing repairs and tourism, rather than branching out into new territory.

Again, this left few examples of significant divergence or innovation. As with education, the National Health Service Reform (Scotland) Act 2003 legitimised existing significant differences by legally abolishing the 'internal market' at a time when the UK government was extending it in England through the introduction of foundation hospitals. This leaves two 'flagship' policies. The first bill reformed local government elections by introducing proportional representation by the single transferable vote (STV). This was a key demand of the Liberal Democrats in coalition negotiations and at the elections in 2007 had a profound effect on the local government landscape, eliminating single-party control almost everywhere and undermining an important support base for the Labour Party. The second introduced a comprehensive ban on smoking in public places, marking significant divergence until Westminster, influenced by events in Scotland, voted for similar legislation a year later.

One consequence of designing the new Scottish Parliament as a departure from 'old Westminster' is that the members' bill process became much simpler and gave many MSPs a reasonable chance of legislative progress or, at the least, a strong agenda-setting tool. Until reforms in 2004, an MSP was given one month from publication of the bill to gather the support of 11 members. If successful, the bill would then go to committee for often extensive deliberations at stage one before being discussed in plenary. The smoking ban represents the best example of this new potential for 'venue shift' to the Scottish Parliament. The members' bill process became a focal point for public health groups dissatisfied with executive policy. Stewart Maxwell MSP introduced a (less comprehensive) bill to ban smoking in public places and gathered widespread support which continued into the extensive health committee stage one consultation and evidence-gathering process. This ability for MSPs and committees to set the agenda during the legislative process is stronger than in Westminster.

Yet, we should not go too far, for three main reasons. First, on the whole, non-executive legislation has been fairly limited in substance, covering 'handout' bills or issues such as post-graduate education at St Andrews, dog fouling, shop opening hours at Christmas and planning issues for land owned by the National Galleries of Scotland. The most high profile bills either took years to pass (fox hunting) or were superseded before being implemented (poindings). Second, MSPs and committees have limited resources with which to pass legislation. Indeed, excessive reliance on the non-executive bills unit (NEBU) prompted reforms in 2004 to increase the support needed (19 MSPs) and in 2005 to tighten the rules on NEBU help, based on size, scope and complexity of proposed bills. Third, after a flurry of excitement in the first session in which 11 members' and committee bills were passed, representing 18% of all legislation, non-executive output fell to three members' bills and one committee bill from 2003-07. Indeed, proportionately, it has fallen to a level consistent with Westminster.

Therefore, if anything, the overall process of legislation from 1999-2007 said much more about the executive-parliament relationship than marking a new dawn in public policy divergence or innovation. The experience from 1999-2007 was that the executive proposed (and amended) the majority of legislation, with the Scottish Parliament performing a fairly traditional scrutiny role. Yet, even this process stretched its resources, with MSPs and committees complaining that the parliament became little more than 'part of the legislative sausage machine', unable to inquire or set its own agenda because of the executive's excessive demands on it and the propensity to change committee numbers and membership throughout.

The Third Session: Minority Government 2007–
In this light, the effect of SNP minority government has been profound. There were two flagship policies requiring legislation. One was to replace the council tax with a local income tax and was abandoned in February 2009 when it became obvious that it would not be possible to assemble a parliamentary majority. The other was a commitment to a referendum on independence which, at the time of writing, looks impossible, although the Scottish Labour leadership has undertaken two U-turns on the issue. Only six Scottish government bills had been passed by January 2009 (plus a members' bill on the register of tartans), including four housekeeping bills initiated by the previous executive (the budget, updating public health and the judiciary, preparing for the Commonwealth Games), a bill abolishing bridge tolls and a bill to abolish the graduate endowment. Most bills in the pipeline are also either inherited or housekeeping (debt and damages, rape and sexual offences, Creative Scotland, flooding), with plans to elect health board members (following an unsuccessful members' bill in 2007) the exception. On public services, the drift of Scotland away from the English model of consumerism and competition has continued and accentuated, occasionally requiring legislation such as that proposed in 2009 to ban private firms from buying health centres.

Given its lack of a majority the SNP administration cannot use legislation as its primary policy vehicle, preferring instead a combination of public expenditure decisions, including an attempt to reject public-private partnerships to finance major capital projects, and an imaginative use of the existing statute book. The legislative process takes much longer, and is dominated by the need to gain multi-party consent, even during the previously routine budget process. The new SNP strategy highlights the fact that primary legislation provides an imperfect picture of public policy decisions. The same was true before the SNP came to power; examples of non-legislative public policy from 1999 to 2007 include the pursuit of social inclusion, largely as a cross-cutting theme to be 'mainstreamed' into departmental portfolios, albeit with a presumption that all legislation would be exclusion-proofed; and rural policy, largely driven by an EU agenda and the use of finance associated with the common agricultural policy.

There has been a less profound SNP effect on the governmental use of legislative consent motions (LCMs, previously called Sewel motions). These were passed frequently by the Scottish Parliament from 1999 to 2007 as a means of giving consent for Westminster to legislate in devolved matters. This provoked a lot of criticism that Holyrood was shirking its responsibilities or deferring too much to the centre. In fact most Sewel motions were on rather technical matters, to block potential loopholes between Scottish and English provision that might be used by criminals, or in some cases to protect Scottish prerogatives in Westminster legislation ('reverse-Sewel'). Passing responsibility for civil partnerships to Westminster, on the other hand, seems to have been the result of political cowardice after the bruising the parliament had received over the repeal of Section 28A on the 'promotion' of homosexuality. The debate on their use heightened during the 2003-07 session – in which the Scottish Green party and the Scottish Socialist party joined the SNP in opposing most on principle – but the procedures committee effectively established the LCM as a routine tool of government in 2005. By April 2007, 79 LCMs (or 10 per year) had been passed. Since May 2007, the SNP government has approved proportionally fewer (10 in 22 months) and has sought, when possible, to promote Scottish parliamentary measures instead, or accept 'reverse-Sewel' motions when offered. However, we have not witnessed the type of sea-change we might have expected.

Devolution has profoundly changed the legislative process in Scotland from one conducted in the specialised committees of Westminster, away both from Scotland and the parliamentary mainstream, to a more open and transparent mode. Interest groups find it much easier to engage and there is more media scrutiny. Holyrood has emulated the Westminster model of government and opposition, and partisan politics dominates the legislative process in contentious matters. On the other hand, on many social and economic issues there are not big differences between the parties and, on non-partisan issues, the committees have provided a vehicle for consensual solutions in a way that is more difficult at Westminster.

Chapter 6

Access and Participation: Aiming High

Bill Thomson

The Scottish Parliament should be accessible, open, responsive, and develop procedures which make possible a participative approach to the development, consideration and scrutiny of policy and legislation.
(Consultative Steering Group)

The aspiration to move to a more open and participative form of parliament, and away from the difficulties of engaging with scrutiny of policy and legislation on Scottish issues at Westminster, posed significant challenges. These were both to the culture of government and to the arcane traditions of parliamentary procedure in a mature, representative democracy. This chapter reviews progress and considers the scope for further developments.

Openness and Accessibility
All proceedings of the parliament are held in public except where committees resolve to meet in private and, in fact, committees conduct the vast bulk of their business in public (e.g. 77% of the 934 committee hours in 2004–05). Anyone can book a ticket to sit in the public gallery during meetings of the parliament and the public business of committee meetings. The only regular exception to the availability of seats in the public galleries is the weekly session of First Minister's questions. This is generally oversubscribed so an overflow gallery with a live broadcast of the proceedings is often required. Public meetings of committees and all chamber business have been recorded and the live feed made available to broadcasters. Video extracts are also available on request. An official report, a substantially verbatim record of what was said, is published. For chamber business, this is available by 8am on the following day.

Visitors to the Scottish Parliament at Holyrood can benefit from the fact that it is housed in a modern, accessible building. Induction loops have been installed in the chamber gallery, on the floor of the chamber, and in all committee rooms. Signage is written in English and in Gaelic, and British Sign Language (BSL) interpreters can be made available on request. For those who simply wish to visit, tours are available in a number of different languages, as are leaflets on the building, the way the parliament works, and how to engage with it. The atmosphere of the main entrance hall is lively with groups of visitors and schoolchildren.

There is, as the following sections show, much evidence of a 'culture' of openness and accessibility which the Consultative Steering Group (CSG) argued should permeate the parliament.

Information

The parliament publishes masses of information, including bills, committee agendas, committee papers for all public business, committee reports, the official report, the minutes of meetings and most of the reports considered by the Scottish Parliamentary Corporate Body (SPCB), information about forthcoming business, research briefings prepared for committees and members, details of expenses claimed by members and much more. So, information is available to those who wish to engage with or to monitor the activities of the parliament. Indeed, for most purposes, the problem is not so much the availability of information as where to find it and how to filter it. All of the material is available on the parliament's website, and is listed in the publication scheme prepared under the Freedom of Information (Scotland) Act 2002. Any member of the public who does not know where to start can contact the parliament's public information service or visit one of the partner libraries.

Committees set and publish their own agendas. Most also give advance notice of future business or publish their forward work programme. The parliament's media relations office works with committees to ensure that this information is available to the national press, and to relevant local and specialist publications. Committees embarking on an inquiry will publish advertisements calling for evidence.

The agenda for chamber business is proposed by the parliamentary bureau which consists of the business managers of the main parties and is chaired by the Presiding Officer. The bureau meets weekly in private, but the business motion proposing a forward agenda for two or three weeks' business is published the following day and, along with any amendments proposed by members, is voted on at a meeting of the parliament. The agreed programme is then published in the following day's business bulletin.

Participation

Only members of the Scottish Parliament, and the law officers, can speak in debates and vote on decisions in the chamber. Non–members may be involved in committee proceedings, if invited to give evidence in an inquiry or in support of a petition. However, there are many ways in which members of the public and community groups, charities, professional and business associations can influence indirectly the business of the parliament. These are generally encouraged by the parliament, its committees and by its members.

Concerns about policies, their impact in practice, or about the performance of public bodies, perceived inequities and suggestions for changes to the law are most commonly raised with individual members of the Scottish Parliament in meetings or in correspondence. The parliament provides funds for members to establish an office in their constituency or region, and to enable members to employ staff to assist with case work and keep in touch with their constituents via correspondence and campaigns. Members hold surgeries in their constituency or region, generally on a weekly basis, and attend public meetings on topics of more general concern. Some constituents travel to Edinburgh to meet members at the parliament. This may take place in private meetings, or at receptions and other events sponsored by members. There are of course demonstrations and other gatherings outside the parliament.

Certain topics of interest have resulted in the formation of 'cross-party groups' which the public can attend. Cross-party groups must comply with rules intended to prevent improper influence being exerted. Sixty-six are currently recognised, on topics as varied as: asylum seekers and refugees, chronic pain, Malawi and Scots contemporary music. Topics discussed in the groups may form the subject of motions for debate in the members' business slot held at the end of each meeting of the parliament. For example, members' business on Wednesday 11 February 2009 was a debate on a motion by Irene Oldfather MSP, which invited the parliament '[to note] the launch of the report, *People with Dementia in NHS Accident and Emergency – Recognising Their Needs*, by the cross-party group on Alzheimer's...'.

As recommended by the CSG, any person or group of people may submit a petition to the Scottish Parliament, intentionally set up to be more participative than the process in Westminster where a member had to sponsor a petition. Petitions can be submitted electronically, as well as in more traditional paper format. E-petitions are published on the web and allow people to add their support electronically or to submit comments on the petition.

All petitions on matters within the competence of the parliament are considered initially by the public petitions committee. The committee may invite the petitioner, or a representative, to address it briefly and it may decide to take evidence. In many cases, the petition will be referred to a minister or public body for a response. Some are referred to the appropriate subject committee for further consideration, particularly if they are relevant to matters on which the committee intends to take evidence, for an inquiry or in the course of considering legislation. For example, the health and sport committee at its meeting on 25 February 2009 took evidence from representatives for three petitions in the course of its pathways into sport inquiry.

Petitions can set the agenda for debate, influence policy reviews and, in some cases, legislation. They are perhaps a good example of power-sharing, the first CSG principle, being put into practice.

Legislation

The CSG report made much of the perceived need to increase participation in the legislative process. The recommendations of the CSG have been closely followed in the drafting of the standing orders which govern legislative and other procedures in the parliament. Thus, bills introduced in the Scottish Parliament require to be accompanied by a policy memorandum setting out:

- The policy objectives of the bill
- Alternatives considered and the reason for preferring the approach taken in the bill
- Consultation undertaken and the results of the consultation
- An assessment of the effects of the bill on equal opportunities, human rights, and other specified matters (standing orders, rule 9.3)

On introduction, bills are referred to a committee which is required to consider and report to the parliament on the general principles of the bill. In doing so, the committee will generally invite written submissions and hear from witnesses on the issues raised in the policy memorandum before submitting their report.

Participation by members of the public and interested bodies is less direct once a bill has passed stage one. The opportunity to influence a bill at stage two or three is limited to suggesting amendments which can be put forward by any member. Amendments are voted on and, until the advent of minority government, generally failed unless supported by the minister in charge of the bill.

The rules of procedure allow committees to meet outside Edinburgh. This has happened on over 100 occasions since 1999. For example, the session two education committee met at Sabhal Mor Ostaig on Skye when considering the Gaelic Language (Scotland) bill and the session three economy, energy and tourism committee met in Aberdeen during its tourism inquiry. Committees have on occasions taken evidence by video link.

Rule 12.7 of the standing orders makes provision for committees to appoint academics and other specialists as advisers 'upon any competent matter'. Advisers tend to be appointed for limited periods to deal with specific issues, and they do not become members of the committee. They therefore have no right to speak at meetings, and they cannot vote. However, this rule does allow for a more in-depth form of participation by some in the proceedings of the committees, and brings external expertise directly to bear on the parliament's deliberations.

Innovations

As already noted, the SPCB, which is responsible for the property, services and staff of the parliament, is committed to encouraging public participation in the work of the parliament. The interim strategic plan adopted in October 2008 sets out three areas for delivery, including public engagement, for which the key outcome is 'increased public awareness of the parliament and engagement with the parliamentary process in Scotland'. Following a review, the education programme was extended in 2008–09, both by doubling the capacity of educational tours and events at Holyrood to accommodate over 29,000 young people and by the appointment of part-time education outreach staff based in areas beyond easy travelling distance to Edinburgh to engage over 12,000 pupils. The parliament has also organised events which are open to particular interest groups and to the wider public.

Since 1999, the parliament has organised four 'business in the parliament' conferences jointly with the Scottish executive/government. Each has been a mixture of plenary sessions held in the chamber and discussion groups, with members, ministers and over 150 invited guests from Scotland's business community nominated by the members of the Scottish Parliament.

The SPCB agreed to the holding of a pilot *Festival of Politics* in August 2005. It took place at Holyrood, making use of the chamber, committee rooms and public spaces, with both ticketed and free events, and a budget (net of sponsorship and ticket income) of £32,500. The event was a great success and has been repeated in each subsequent year. Additional attractions have included the staging of the world press photo exhibition in the main hall of the parliament for a period overlapping with the festival and, in August 2008, a pioneering collaboration with the Carnegie UK and Dunfermline trusts to bring forward a range of events at both the Carnegie festival in Dunfermline and at Holyrood.

Developments
The SPCB recently agreed a contract for the re-design of the parliament's website, once hailed as a leading example. This is in recognition of the need to improve access to information on the parliament and its activities, the accessibility of the website itself, and with a view to exploring the opportunities for engagement and participation presented by technological advances. Members of the public and other users of the website are being involved in the design process.

Among the events planned by the SPCB to mark the 10th anniversary of the devolving of powers to the Scottish Parliament is a community partnership project. This is a pilot to be run in partnership with community groups who have contacts with groups who are currently under-represented in engaging with parliamentary processes: ethnic minorities, disability rights organisations and difficult to reach young people. The objective is to provide assistance and information to allow the groups to have their voices heard more effectively in the parliament.

The public petitions committee, aware of the need to increase awareness and encourage broader participation, has instituted an inquiry into the petitions process.

Reflection

A number of criticisms have been made of the CSG's advocacy of a new form of consensus politics, different from the traditional, adversarial approach at Westminster, characterised by opportunities for access and participation, and leading to a sharing of power between the executive, the legislature and the people. Arguably, that vision ignores the reality of party politics in Scotland and fails to take account of the inevitable limitations on participation within a system of representative democracy. Some commentators see a pattern of development of new forms of governance in devolved and regional political arrangements, bringing expectations of and experiments in participation and power-sharing, along with the risk of blurring lines of accountability.

Against that background, and perhaps notwithstanding the risks and the difficulties, there is evidence to show that the Scottish Parliament is prepared to go to some lengths to extend the opportunities for participation beyond the usual suspects. It is, of course, too early to make any assessment of the success of the pilot projects or to know the outcome of the petitions inquiry. However, the fact that the parliament is prepared to commit resources to challenging the current boundaries of participation suggests that the spirit of the CSG recommendations lives on and that there is a willingness to move the bar to an even higher level.

Chapter 7

Travelling the Distance? Equal Opportunities and the Scottish Parliament

Fiona Mackay

Introduction: Travelling the Distance
Equal opportunities (EO) plays a paradoxical role in the post-devolution politics of Scotland. On the one hand, it is a touchstone of 'new politics' – and a key principle of the Scottish Parliament. On the other, it is formally beyond the Scottish Parliament – one of the powers reserved to Westminster – with a couple of concessionary exceptions to the reservation, which can appear confusing and limiting. This paper considers how – and how well – EO has 'travelled the distance'[1] in the Scottish Parliament over the last decade: in its core business, and as an employer and a service provider.

In the absence of any recent systematic study looking at the operation of EO in the parliament, this piece is necessarily broad brush. I argue that despite shortfalls, slippages and setbacks, overall there is a positive story to tell.

Building EO 'in with the Bricks': Hard and Soft Measures
Defining equal opportunities is easier said than done. EO is most directly associated with legal and procedural models, concerned with anti-discrimination, equal treatment and the creation of a level playing field. But the term EO has also served as an umbrella for other, more expansive understandings of equalities, for example the active promotion of equality, inclusion and diversity as social goods and goals, the 'mainstreaming' of equalities perspectives into policy-making, the linking of equalities and democratic participation, and change goals in terms of concrete outcomes. In post-devolution Scotland, minimalist, formal and legal understandings of EO co-exist in tension with expansive and aspirational ideas, with often confusing consequences.

There were two potential ways in which EO could have been 'built in with the bricks' of the Scottish Parliament. 'Hard' measures relate to legal powers to legislate, regulate and the ability to enforce compliance and accountability; whilst soft measures relate to building commitment and shared norms, through informal (in the sense of not legally binding) rules and practices,

---

[1] I take my title from a striking artwork on display at Holyrood. *Travelling the Distance* by Shauna McMullan represents the inclusion of women in public spaces and highlights the importance of cultural expression as well as legal and political measures, in promoting norms and aspirations. My thanks to Ann Henderson, Angela O'Hagan and Rona Fitzgerald for comments at short notice on an earlier draft of this chapter; to editors Charlie Jeffery and James Mitchell; and to the equalities stakeholders who took time to share their views. All mistakes and misunderstandings are my own.

awareness-raising and so on. Accountability takes the form of answerability, rather than enforceability.

Turning first to 'hard' measures: campaigners failed in their bid for EO powers to be devolved. EO is listed in the Scotland Act 1998 as one of the powers reserved to the UK Parliament. The lobbying of equality groups and women activists did result in the insertion of two 'exceptions' to the reservation. The Scottish Parliament has the power: 1) to encourage (other than by prohibition or regulation) equal opportunities, and in particular the observance of equal opportunity requirements; and 2) to impose duties on public bodies to ensure they have due regard to equal opportunities requirements.

EO is defined in the Act as 'the prevention, elimination or regulation of discrimination between persons on grounds of sex, or marital status, on racial grounds, or on grounds of disability, age, sexual orientation, language or social origin, or of other personal attributes, including beliefs or opinions, such as religious beliefs and political opinions'. This covered many more strands than the EO legislation of the time and has given the Scottish Parliament the scope to pursue an expansive multi-strand approach, for example through the mainstreaming of LGBT (lesbian, gay, bisexual and transgender) issues. But the EO *requirements* are more restricted, and refer to groups then covered by anti-discrimination legislation in various acts of parliament.

Legal regulatory powers are only one side of the coin. The second approach centres on 'softer' measures, in particular, the inclusion of EO 'for all' as one of the four founding principles of the Scottish Parliament as proposed in the CSG blueprint report. The institutional 'blueprints' of the parliament contained important statements and mechanisms for promoting equal opportunities. Unsurprisingly, given the role of women's organisations and feminist ideas in devolution campaigns, issues of gender equality were initially prominent. Key features included: 'family friendly' working hours for the parliament and the recognition of Scottish school holidays; a purpose-built visitors' crèche; a parliamentary equal opportunities committee with a remit for equal opportunities issues both inside and outside the parliament; an equality unit within the Scottish executive, tasked with promoting multiple strands of equality; the commitment of both parliament and the executive to 'mainstreaming' equality – including gender equality – across all their areas of work including legislation and policy-making; and the requirement that memoranda accompanying executive bills include an equal opportunities impact statement. The other key principles have provided enabling conditions for the promotion of EO through more open, accessible decision-making processes and more participatory politics.

EO and the Parliament: Legal Duties, Champions and Mainstreaming
Why are equal opportunities powers important? In short, because most of the

areas devolved to the Scottish Parliament have equalities dimensions: health, housing, education, policing and justice, economic development. The parliament has used its powers under the exceptions to the reservations to impose general equality duties on public bodies. Some 14 Scottish acts to date – ranging from the Standards in Scotland's Schools etc. Act in 2000 to the Planning Scotland Act 2006 – have placed duties on public authorities to encourage the observance of equal opportunities requirements. These authorities include Scottish ministers, local authorities, education authorities, social landlords, NHS trusts and mental health officers. In addition, some public authorities have been required to prepare strategies setting out how they will encourage equal opportunities.

However, legal uncertainty as to the scope of the reservations, and political timidity about bumping up against the devolution settlement have been stumbling blocks to the use of powers. In evidence given by the Equality and Human Rights Commission (Scotland) to the parliament's EO committee in 2008, 'There is no authoritative source that provides a clear and accessible explanation of the Scottish Parliament's equal opportunity powers and what they mean in practice.' Furthermore, confusion over the meaning of EO has constrained those seeking to promote an expansive rather than a minimalist anti-discrimination agenda. The equal opportunities committee reported in 2008 that this creates 'a mindset that believes that achieving equal opportunities is about preventing or eliminating discrimination and nothing else ... how a policy can promote equality of opportunity and good relations – those positive aspects seem to have been lost'. There has been no assessment to date of the effectiveness of the legal duties introduced, but they appear in many cases to have been hobbled by poor integration and specification, the absence of clear monitoring arrangements and the non-enforcement of reporting requirements. The question also needs to be asked: is the power to legislate – without the ability to regulate – a power worth possessing?

Meanwhile, there have been significant developments at Westminster in equal opportunities legislation since 1999. New race, disability and gender equality public sector duties (which came into force in 2002, 2006 and 2007 respectively) contain 'positive' duties that go beyond anti-discrimination to require public authorities actively to: promote equality; foster good relations and positive attitudes; eliminate harassment; draw up equality schemes; and consider and consult on how policies may impact upon equality (see www.equalityhumanrights.com). Under Scottish powers, the legislation has been tailored for Scotland. There are additional specific requirements, for example the disability duty and gender duty each require Scottish ministers to report regularly on progress and outline priorities. It can be argued that the new public sector equality duties are more permissive and expansive than earlier generations of equality legislation; more in keeping with the aspirational ideas of equality underpinning the parliament's founding principles and the Scottish executive's Equality Strategy 2000. Nonetheless, the results of recent developments can be seen a further recipe for confusion: public bodies have multiple sets of equality requirements – one regulated to meet the new equality duties around race, disability and gender; others unregulated to encourage equal opportunities across narrow and broad strands outlined in the 1998 Scotland Act.

Mainstreaming and the EO Committee

The second major approach relates to the 'soft' measures of mainstreaming of equal opportunities into the parliament's legislative and scrutiny functions, as set out by the CSG. The equal opportunities committee was created as a mandatory committee, in order to act as a champion for equal opportunities and a catalyst to facilitate good practice across the parliament. However, parliamentary committees have been reluctant to take responsibility for equal opportunities in their areas of expertise, and have tended to leave mainstreaming analysis to the EO committee. Despite repeated endorsements of the mainstreaming approach and the provision of mainstreaming guidelines, committees remain unlikely to explicitly address the equalities or equal opportunities dimensions of their subject area or to make links between their own work and that of the EO committee. In part, this lack of cross-committee working on issues of equality has been the result of the sheer volume of legislative activity in the first two sessions, which has constrained the capacity for creative working across boundaries. There are discussions within the parliament about whether a duty to address equalities issues should be incorporated formally into each committee's terms of reference to provide a mechanism to promote the 'mainstreaming' of mainstreaming.

After a slow start, the EO committee is generally regarded to have gained in confidence and expertise. Early successes in session one included the championing of the repeal of Section 28A and pioneering outreach events, for example with the gypsy-traveller community and young people. In session two, the committee became more assertive, for instance in its scrutiny of the equalities implications of the annual budget, a wide-ranging disability inquiry and a review of progress of equalities in Scotland. In session three, the committee has continued its work on the budget as well as focusing on equal pay, amongst other matters. Successful relationships have been established with its external constituency, according to stakeholders. Internally, however, it is perceived to be isolated and undervalued: something of a 'back water' despite the espoused importance of the principle of EO by the parliament as a whole.

Bringing EO Home: The Parliament as an Employer and Service Provider

The duty to encourage EO might be expected to begin at home. Over the decade of devolution, the Scottish Parliamentary Corporate Body (SPCB) and executive of the Scottish Parliament have responded to internal and external pressures, and worked with trade unions and other bodies, to build up a track record of good EO practice in employment. The SPCB has also linked the access and participation agenda with equal opportunities, seeking to create and promote inclusion.

There is much evidence that the SPCB and executive of the Scottish Parliament take EO seriously. An equality policy framework has been in place since 2001, with specialist equalities staff, comprehensive policies, clear lines of responsibility and reporting, annual equality reports, and biennial equality staff audits. A range of good practice employment policies is in place, including flexible working and support for childcare. All parliamentary staff undergo mandatory equalities training. The SPCB has also provided guidance on EO issues and employment rights with regards to MSPs' staff (for whom it is not responsible).

Comprehensive schemes on disability, gender and race, have been drawn up in response to the new – or strengthened – public sector equality duties. Annual reports stress the need to avoid complacency and continue to make progress. External plaudits include an independent equal pay audit, carried out in 2004, which revealed no evidence of gender pay differentials; and the former equal opportunities commission has used the parliament's approach to integrating equality considerations into the procurement process as a best practice case study.

EO considerations in service delivery are also flagged up as part of wider concerns with making the parliament accessible and inclusive, which is in turn part of the wider project of building legitimacy and support for the parliament. The parliament's equality framework states that, 'Promoting equal opportunities is not an optional add-on to our work, and it is about more than just complying with the relevant pieces of legislation. [...] equal opportunities must be central to all of our efforts to maximise the effectiveness of the parliament and the impact of devolution in Scotland.'

The parliament has staged exhibitions, events and activities targeted at marginalised groups as well as working to ensure that services are accessible to all. However, there are concerns that commitment to EO remains contingent and can slip off the agenda. The failure of the parliament to highlight and publicise its evident achievements and initiatives, as an EO employer and service provider, suggests that the principle may not be so highly regarded internally after all. For example, despite its groundbreaking status, the future of the parliamentary crèche has been repeatedly placed in doubt, in the context of competing demands for space. MSPs and staff, mostly but not exclusively women, have had to lobby repeatedly over the decade: first, to ensure the planned crèche did not fall victim to cost cutting in the early days; and latterly, to demand the facility is supported and adequately promoted.

Looking Like Scotland? Gender Balance and Diversity

The Scottish Parliament had aspirations to 'look like' Scotland. The high proportion of women MSPs returned in the first elections provided a powerful and visible shorthand for EO and the 'new politics' more generally. Similarly, the more-or-less equal numbers of female and male parliamentary staff (excluding MSPs' staff) reinforces the vision of inclusivity (although men are over-represented in top grades; and disabled persons and black and minority ethnic people remain under-represented in the workforce).

Responsibility for gender balance in political recruitment and selection and the fair representation of minority groups lies, of course, with political parties not the parliament. However, the decrease in female MSPs from 39.5% in 2003 to 34.1% in 2007 (rising to 35.4 % in 2009) sounds a warning against complacency: progress can be reversed. The death in 2009 of Scotland's first minority ethnic MSP Bashir Ahmad (elected in 2007) means that the political face of the parliament is once again all-white. The link between 'being there' (the presence of women, black and minority ethnic people, disabled people and so on) and 'making a difference' (in terms of equality-seeking behaviour) is far from straightforward. However, there is evidence that, in the early years, a more gender-balanced parliament contributed to a reprioritisation of equalities issues, and concrete policy outcomes such as equality proofing budget processes and action on domestic abuse. These impacts relate not only to the presence and actions of gender equality and equal opportunities champions, mostly women but with some notable men; but also to the more general 'new politics' ethos of the parliament.

Conclusions: A Distance Travelled, a Distance to Travel

A decade on, there is widespread confusion about the scope and extent of the Scottish Parliament's powers with respect to EO. For some, the devolution settlement provides a constraint and it has taken determination and creativity to progress the agenda: 'I think that the parliament and equality movements have done well in finding so many ways to make equal opportunities the business of devolved government.' For other stakeholders it is the case that, parliamentarians, lawyers and civil servants have been timid and short-sighted, 'there is always a lack of confidence in taking on a progressive, permissive equalities agenda and pushing the powers and taking expansive view of Scotland Act'.

The question of whether or not EO/equalities powers should be devolved is part of the ongoing discussions of the National Conversation and the Calman Commission on the future of devolution. However, further thought also is needed to figure out how to make the most of existing powers in a complicated landscape of equalities duties. The introduction of post-legislative scrutiny and monitoring are seen by many as particularly necessary to 'follow through' on legislation and major policy programmes, and in order to scrutinise implementation and assess equalities outcomes.

We know that equalities initiatives tend to be 'carried' in the sense of the need to coincide or be congruent with other public policy or political objectives. The continued resonance of the founding principle of 'equal opportunities for all' lies, at least in part, with its links with inclusiveness, wider participation and democratic legitimacy. EO is not always central, it is often marginalised, but it remains a touchstone. Equalities activists consulted for this piece argued that parliamentarians and officials consider themselves 'answerable' – a soft form of accountability – on matters of EO. In this respect, it has 'travelled the distance' to date.

It is not my intention to argue that soft laws, instruments and accountabilities are sufficient for progressing equalities. Recent survey evidence underscores the complexity of social attitudes about equalities and the slow pace of change. Nonetheless, shared values and informal norms are powerful ways in which institutions, such as the Scottish Parliament, are 'lived' on a day-to-day basis and play an important part in how agendas are sustained over time. Despite shortfalls, slippages and setbacks, overall there is a relatively positive story to tell. EO remains a principle with mobilising power in the parliament, its practices and its dealings with civil society, the public and its staff. However, there is still a distance to travel: there is confusion about the scope and capacity to act around EO, tension between expansive and minimalist conceptions of equality, and concerns about faltering commitment and competing priorities as the parliament enters its second decade.

Chapter 8

Parliamentary Accountability: Aspiration or Reality?

Chris Himsworth

I assure all colleagues present that "blah" – the answer from Jim Mather to a recent parliamentary question from Annabel Goldie – was a genuine mistake. It was inadvertent and was not a pilot for our new approach to parliamentary accountability. [Interruption.] Mr Swinney is saying that I should not rule out such an approach at this stage.
(Rt Hon Alex Salmond MSP, 18 June 2008)

Then and Now
One of the effects of the passing of the 10 years since the establishment of the Scottish Parliament is that it has become a part of the 'normal' structure of governance in the country – so 'normal', in fact, that it is becoming difficult to recall how very strange things were before the great devolutionary stride of 1999. If one of the strangest and most unsatisfactory gaps had been the lack of a Scotland-based law-maker, the second most important omission was the almost complete absence of mechanisms for holding to account those who wielded executive authority in the country. By that, of course, we meant, at that time, the secretary of state for Scotland and his or her small team of junior ministers, including the Scottish law officers. Their civil servants in the Scottish Office were, for the most part, located in Scotland but their parliamentary accountability was to the physically distant Westminster Parliament. Under the doctrine of ministerial responsibility, ministers were held to account under the procedures of that parliament. Questions (both oral and written) could be asked and had to be answered by ministers. The select committee for Scottish affairs could pursue inquiries in which ministers would again be answerable for their policies and decisions. Other fora included the Scottish grand committee and, on Scottish bills, the Scottish standing committees. In a scaled-down version these accountability mechanisms still perform their tasks in relation to the much smaller ministerial team under the secretary of state and the very much smaller Scotland Office.

But, as a means for the scrutiny of the general range of executive authority in Scotland, these forms of accountability in the Westminster Parliament were distant, limited and inadequate. With the arrival of the Scotland Act's new Scottish executive in 1999 came the Scottish Parliament's big challenge and opportunity. The number of ministers had expanded greatly, their powers likewise. The opportunities for a strong response from MSPs, in terms of their numbers, their resources, and the time available to them had also expanded.

The engagement between the two would be one of the most important features of the life of the new parliament. In a formal sense, it was broadly the same system of parliamentary government with, at its core, the principle of ministerial responsibility which was to be established at Holyrood and this has indeed been expressly articulated in the Scottish ministerial code which states that: 'Ministers have a duty to the parliament to account, and be held to account, for the policies, decisions and actions taken within their field of responsibility.'

The question, however, was how successful this quest for the parliamentary accountability of ministers would be. The specific defects of the pre-1999 Scottish mechanisms at Westminster could probably be quite readily overcome. The much greater challenge was that of making accountability work at all. The track record, both at Westminster and elsewhere, has been one of failure. Executive power has increased. Executive domination of legislatures has increased. The power of legislatures to exercise their allotted role of holding to account has undergone a long-term decline. There are several reasons for this but, at the core – seen by some as rotten – is the political control (exercisable largely through the dominant political party) in the hands of party leaders, especially the Prime Minister or equivalent, over the party membership whose formal responsibility, paradoxically, is the holding to account of that same party leadership.

The question for the Scottish Parliament was whether it had a new opportunity to buck that trend and to succeed where others had failed. That remains the key question today. Has the parliament succeeded?

Accountability Rules and Principles
If there was to be a successful outcome, this might have been sought in two principal sources – on the one hand, the formal rules contained in the Scotland Act itself and, secondly, the parliament's own commitment to the task and the use to which it might put its available powers and influence to change the pervading culture of executive domination.

The reason for placing an initial emphasis on the Scotland Act is that it did indeed introduce at least two significant changes affecting the standard model of accountability at Westminster. The first was the introduction of the additional member system of proportional representation in Scottish Parliament elections. A consequence which was foreseen from the outset was that the chances of single party dominance in the parliament were very greatly reduced. In turn, this was almost certain to redress the balance between the parliament and the executive. Coalition conditions such as those experienced in the first two sessions of the parliament made government discipline less easy to maintain and, therefore, strengthened the power of parliament and its capacity to hold the executive to account. Even more, this has been the case in the minority government conditions of the third session. When a government has no guaranteed overall majority it is forced to be more responsive. An illustration has been the manoeuvring required to gain support for the government's budget bills – a phenomenon unknown under conditions of single-party control at Westminster.

The other change built into the constitution of the Scottish Parliament was its fixed term. No First Minister, whatever the party political conditions over which he or she presides, has the power unilaterally to terminate the parliament and demand a general election. In turn, this gives the First Minister less political control over the party or coalition of parties which he or she leads than the UK Prime Minister who has a greater opportunity to bring MPs into line with the threat of a general election.

Beyond these constitutional rules, it was made clear from the outset that those who guided the parliament into existence, from the Scottish Constitutional Convention to the Consultative Steering Group, and then the parliament itself in its commitment to its 'founding principles' (reviewed by the parliament's procedures committee in 2003) were dedicated to ensuring that the parliament's accountability functions should be established and thereafter sustained. This was to be a significant component of the 'new politics' which were to characterise the relationships of partnership and participation of devolved governance. Probably these were over-ambitious aspirations from the start. The success or otherwise of the parliament's accountability mechanisms would be a good barometer.

The Record in Practice
As one considers the parliamentary contribution, however, one must also bear in mind that the parliament does not act alone. In particular, the courts, with their role enhanced by new powers under the Human Rights Act 1998, have the high responsibility of imposing accountability to the law. Judicial review in the Court of Session has a lead role here and, although there may be some overlap between the subject matter of judicial review and the political concerns of the parliament, the procedures deployed are quite separate.

Other mechanisms of accountability, however, do give a direct role to the parliament while placing primary responsibility elsewhere. The auditor general for Scotland superintends the procedures for the financial accountability of public authorities (including the Scottish government) but his reports are laid before the parliament and are the subject of inquiry and review by the parliament's public audit committee. In a rather similar way, the Scottish public services ombudsman reviews public sector decision-making against the yardsticks of maladministration and service failure. The ombudsman contributes to enhancing accountability at all the levels of government supervised by the office but, among these, are the departments or directorates of the Scottish government which the parliament has a direct responsibility to hold to account. In addition, the annual reports of the ombudsman are laid before the parliament and it has become the practice of the local government and communities committee (the local government and transport committee before that) to invite the ombudsman to discuss her office's annual report.

Both of these 'indirect' forms of accountability have their general equivalent at Westminster, as do most, but not all, of the other more direct parliamentary mechanisms at Holyrood. Most prominent are the facilities for MSPs to put questions (both oral and written) to ministers; the work of Holyrood's subject committees; and the opportunities for plenary debates, whether at the instigation of opposition parties or individual MSPs as members' business. Chamber debates are held on the forward legislative programmes of governments but also, in the post-decision time period on a wide range of constituency and other concerns, in the manner of adjournment debates at Westminster.

As for parliamentary questions to ministers, the impact of the arrival of the Scottish Parliament has been the big increase in the volume of questions. The much greater number of MSPs, compared with their counterparts as Scottish MPs at Westminster, together with the greater number of ministers (most questions are addressed to the all-compassing 'Scottish executive') have ensured that there is no doubt at all that the burden of questions on ministers and upon the civil servants on whom ministers rely for their replies has greatly increased. The separate sessions for First Minister's questions (on Thursdays at 12 noon) have broadly followed the pattern of weekly questions to the Prime Minister at Westminster.

The major innovation regarding the work of the committees at Holyrood has been the combination of the work of the scrutiny of administration and the scrutiny of bills and statutory instruments within the responsibility of the same committees. The 'subject' committees (e.g. economy, energy and tourism; health and sport etc) which perform the work of select committees at Westminster also take on the role of the 'lead committee' (in almost all cases – there are also occasional ad hoc committees for this purpose) on bills and review subordinate legislation on 'merits' grounds. The argument in favour of this combination of roles in terms of the focusing of expertise and, therefore, the overall rationality of the system are compelling, especially in the light of the expanded role of committees (including that of the subordinate legislation committee) at stage one on bills. There can be little doubt that the systematic re-examination of the case for a bill (including the hearing of evidence from relevant ministers as well as from outsiders) and the accountability function which that discharges represent a big advance on Westminster's halting efforts in this direction.

As an aside, however, it may be wondered whether stage two scrutiny by subject committees has been so impressive. Perhaps it is that committees which have discharged their stage one responsibilities tend to reduce their efforts at stage two? A recent example might be proceedings on the Judiciary and Courts (Scotland) Bill where the justice committee conducted a sustained stage one inquiry. Stage two proceedings in that committee were, however, dispatched in just under two hours. There seems to be less enthusiasm for the prolonged section by section engagement and contestation familiar at Westminster. A good question is whether a measure of accountability is lost in the process.

Turning to the more routine work of the subject committees in 'select committee' mode, their remit (following broadly the lines of their Westminster counterparts) is to consider and report on matters in their subject area within the responsibility of the relevant cabinet secretary. These powers have been deployed to produce significant reports on, among many other things, accessing drugs for cancer patients and the effective use of police resources.

Perhaps the biggest single innovation made when the institutional arrangements at Holyrood were established was that of the creation of the public petitions committee and its procedures for the handling of petitions from members of the public in Scotland. The committee is designed to reflect other parliamentary values – such as access and participation – as much as accountability itself. Indeed, in a constitutional system which relies on the principle of ministerial responsibility and the standard parliamentary mechanisms for upholding that principle, a separate right of citizen access to the parliament, might, on grounds of accountability alone, be thought to be superfluous. However, it is in practice the case that access to the parliament and, therefore, to ministers and the administration by way of petition does often provide an alternative vehicle of accountability.

Another post-1999 innovation – this time, one shared with the UK level – has been the enactment of freedom of information legislation, in the case of Scotland the Freedom of Information (Scotland) Act 2002. At the heart of the quest for accountability is the quest for information and it is clear that the principal purpose of most parliamentary mechanisms (pre-eminently, the parliamentary question) has been, historically, the pursuit of information about government and its processes by parliamentarians. Now, the FoI Act places at the disposal not only of MSPs but also of the citizenry at large a very powerful information-seeking weapon whose consequences have probably yet to be fully realised.

Better than Westminster?
The question posed at the beginning of this paper was whether the Scottish Parliament might succeed in achieving a significant degree of executive accountability where Westminster and others have failed. In my view, despite the passing of 10 years, it is too early to say. And the position has been greatly complicated by the shift from an assessment of the accountability of coalition

governments to the accountability of a minority government. The starting assumption might have been that a minority government would have been especially responsive and accountable because of its constant need to seek renewed parliamentary support for its programme. On the other hand, a rather stark conclusion may be that, because of the restrictions imposed on them by the parliamentary arithmetic, minority governments simply do less and have less to be accountable for.

An accountability audit is, in any event, not a matter of precise calculation. One cannot, for instance, satisfactorily measure accountability according to the number of critical committee reports, the number of votes of no confidence proposed or carried, or the number of government bills lost in the legislative process. Rather, the evaluation required is a softer art. Have the forms of parliamentary procedure triumphed over the underlying substance of executive dominance? It is a question of whether an overall culture of accountability and responsiveness has been achieved and, if so, whether primarily at the hand of the Scottish Parliament or, for instance, at the hand of extra-parliamentary agencies such as *Newsnight Scotland* and the Freedom of Information Act. Maybe it is still too early to say but, if a provisional judgment has to be offered, it would be that that cultural shift has not yet taken place and that the Parliament's accountability mechanisms have fallen far short of the aspirations of the 'new politics'.

Chapter 9

The Principle of Power-Sharing, 10 Years On

Joyce McMillan

They say that every constitutional settlement carries the stamp of the age in which it was born; and history is certainly not short of examples to support the argument. In the unwritten constitution that governs the affairs of Westminster government, it's still possible to detect the preferences and prejudices of a powerful 17th century mercantile and landowning class who were not democrats in any modern sense, but who hated the idea of absolute monarchy, as practised in parts of continental Europe. And the great founding documents of the American Revolution are shaped by a profound New World distaste for the aristocratic hierarchies and privileges around which most European societies were structured.

So it is perhaps not surprising that, in a modest way, the founding principles of the Scottish Parliament also bear the stamp of the times in which they were written, and reflect the priorities of those who were moved to political and civic activism during the 1990s, towards the end of 18 years of Conservative government at Westminster. Twelve years on, it is of course difficult to recall the extent to which the abuses of executive power now associated with long-term New Labour government were, at that time, laid entirely at the door of John Major's unpopular Tory administration, and of Margaret Thatcher's governments before that.

But word for word and allegation for allegation, they were accused of the same attitudes, and the same patterns of behaviour. They were accused of excessive secrecy, and of abusing the idea of freedom of information in order to preserve secrecy. They were accused of corruption in parliament, with junior parliamentarians accepting cash for favours. They were accused of manipulating official statistics for electoral advantage. They were accused of excessive centralisation, and of humiliating Britain's once-mighty centres of local government by turning them into agencies of Westminster. And they were accused of treating parliament itself with contempt: of bullying backbenchers into compliance, of curtailing debate, and of making major ministerial announcements to the media rather than to the Commons. In 1988, a group of centre-left writers and thinkers had launched Charter 88, a UK constitutional reform movement openly modelled on East European citizen campaigns like the Czech Charter 77, which sought to challenge the arbitrary power of the failing communist governments of the old Soviet bloc. The theory was the British constitution had decayed to the point where executive power was excessive, overcentralised, widely abused, and often exercised without sensitivity to the fact that under the first-past-the-post electoral system, governments may win large majorities at Westminster while being rejected by a majority of voters. And parliament, it was felt, had long since lost any real power to control the actions of government.

Power-Sharing in the Home Rule Movement

It was out of this moment, and this particular and widespread centre-left analysis of the flaws in Britain's system of government, that the 1990's movement for Scottish home rule was born, with the founding of the Scottish Constitutional Convention in the spring of 1989; and it is therefore not surprising that the first principle laid down for the new Scottish Parliament – the one most cherished by the convention's convener Canon Kenyon Wright, and the one most likely to prove controversial – enshrined the idea of power-sharing as central to any new age of good governance in Scotland. The idea encompassed both power-sharing between the executive and parliament, and power-sharing between parliament, executive and people; the aim was to usher in a new culture of civility, dialogue and participatory democracy, which would make the crude majoritarian arrogance of the Westminster model a thing of the past.

Nor was the home rule movement short of ideas on how the new power-sharing ethos might be made to work. Ever since 1991, when the Scottish Constitutional Convention had invited Professor Bernard Crick and David Millar to draft an ideal set of standing orders for the new parliament – published under the title *To Make The Scottish Parliament A Model For Democracy* – the movement had been full of debate about new models of representation and participation for the 21st century.

In terms of the rebalancing of power between parliament and executive, it was widely assumed, for example, that in a parliament elected by proportional representation, governing parties would not be able to indulge in the kind of winner-takes-all behaviour commonly seen at Westminster. It was further proposed that Scottish Parliament committees should be more powerful than their Westminster equivalents, with the power to initiate legislation should they think it necessary. And the mechanisms for arranging parliamentary business were to be taken out of the hands of the two leading parties – the notorious 'usual channels' of the Westminster model – and handled instead by an openly elected business committee, on which all the parliament's party interests would be represented.

It was in the area of rebalancing between parliament, executive and people, though, that the thinking around the convention was most ambitious, if also more vague. It is worth noting that there was, in the first place, a strong presumption that the setting up of a Scottish Parliament – as a reflection of Scotland's increasingly strong sense of national identity, and as a significant new tier of government much closer to the people than Westminster – would in itself strengthen the relationship between politicians and people, and encourage higher levels of participation. It was also believed that a proportional system of election would 'make every vote count', reduce voter alienation, and provide a parliament which would seem closer to the people, in that it would reflect the real balance of public opinion. And steps were taken – most obviously in the Labour Party – to ensure that the parliament would contain a substantial proportion of women. Once again, it was believed, with some reason, that a parliament with a more 'normal' gender balance than Westminster – the first Scottish Parliament of 1999 was more than 38% female – would be seen as more accessible to the people, and more representative of them.

Then at the more detailed level, the Crick-Millar proposals had included some concrete practical ideas for improving public involvement in the work of parliament. Among them was the public petitions system which operates in the Scottish Parliament today, in an updated version, and which has been widely admired as a model of its kind. There was, likewise, a strong determination that the new parliament would be at the forefront of the communications revolution that was beginning to sweep the world in the 1990s, and would use state-of-the-art email and internet technology to link parliamentarians to the people.

Beyond all those measures, though, there were also hopes, particularly among the leadership of the Constitutional Convention, that the parliament might, in some structural way, seek to work in partnership with Scottish civil society, which had played such a key role in campaigning for its introduction. During the life of the Constitutional Convention, the then general secretary of the Scottish trades union congress, Campbell Christie – who was one of the convention's prime movers – had also been chairing the Scottish Civic Assembly, which ran alongside the convention, but focused on social and economic issues; and when, after 1999, Christie became the founding convener of the new Scottish Civic Forum, he cherished the idea of some kind of formal agreement between the forum, the parliament and the Scottish executive. Indeed in 2001, the finance minister in the devolved Scottish administration, Angus McKay, actually signed a 'concordat' with the Scottish Civic Forum, offering continued Scottish executive funding in return for the representation of the views of Scottish civil society to the government and parliament. Along with other senior members of the Constitutional Convention, Christie was also appointed by Donald Dewar, secretary of state for Scotland in Tony Blair's first government after 1997, to sit on the 1998-99 Consultative Steering Group (CSG) which would draw up draft procedures for the new parliament; and the convention group on the CSG also pressed strongly for the parliament's standing orders to enshrine closer formal links with civil society.

Power-Sharing in Practice: The Record so Far

In Parliament

The ideas which underpinned the new parliament's principle of power-sharing therefore ranged from ambitious hopes for a radical change in political culture, to very practical measures designed to guarantee high numbers of women MSPs, or to set up an effective petitions system; and it is perhaps not surprising that in practice, the record of success in implementing those ideas has been extremely uneven.

In terms of a rebalancing of powers between parliament and the executive, most observers would probably say that the outcome has been disappointing. The introduction of proportional representation and the consequent negotiation of coalition agreements between Labour and the Liberal Democrats, which characterised the first two Scottish Parliaments of 1999 and 2003, was certainly a novelty in the British party system. But it made barely a dent on the consciousness of Westminster or of the UK parties; and even at Holyrood, the party-political culture remained depressingly unreconstructed, with those who had been involved in the civic and constitutional movements of the 1990s regularly voicing complaints about the persistence or recurrence at Holyrood of bad Westminster habits, including mindless adversarialism, infantile point-scoring at question time, and the fierce whipping of backbench votes, often against individual conscience.

Since the election of May 2007, when the SNP emerged as the largest single party and formed a minority government, it is probably true to say that Scotland has become more aware of the advantages – both democratic and theatrical – of a proportionally-elected parliament in which no one party dominates. But unless the opposition parties are united, and prepared to fight an additional election at any time, executive power remains difficult to challenge on most issues.

And if proportional representation has not weakened executive power to the extent some had expected, the Scottish Parliament committees have also, in general, proved weaker than the architects of devolution originally hoped, undermined by the small size of the parliament, and by the consequent high turnover both in the membership of committees, and in the chairing of them. In the first parliament of 1999-2003, the dissident Labour MSP John McAllion became something of a 'star' committee chair, as convener of the first petitions committee. But the Scottish Parliament has yet to produce a Gwyneth Dunwoody or a John McFall: a long-term committee chair famous for resistance to executive power, and for asking the right tough questions. And parliamentary business remains largely a matter agreed among the largest parties, although in a slightly less shadowy way than at Westminster.

Power-Sharing with the People

When it comes to power-sharing with the people, though, the picture is far more complex. In the broadest sense, the idea that people living in Scotland would feel closer to a devolved government in Edinburgh has probably been vindicated. Those organised groups and agencies in Scottish society which are actively engaged with government and parliament have been through a decade of intensive lobbying and consultation at both parliamentary and executive levels, and clearly, in most cases, enjoy greater access to government, and greater influence on policy-making, than they did before 1999.

For these groups – and for the vast numbers of school parties, civic groups and individuals who have visited the parliament in person or electronically since 1999 – the parliament's efforts to make itself accessible and interactive have paid off; although 10 years on, other parliaments are now beginning to equal and surpass Holyrood's efforts at e-democracy. Even for the vast disaffected majority, who view national politics through the prism of the popular media, there is evidence – as researchers at Edinburgh University put it, a few years after devolution – that if the modern relationship between people and politicians is that of the dog to the lamp-post, then for most Scots, the Scottish Parliament has become the lamp-post of choice.

It is worth noting, though, that none of these factors have been sufficient to overcome the pervasive disaffection from formal politics, and active mistrust of party politicians, that has become one of the defining attitudes of our age. Despite the growth of Scottish national feeling, despite the fact that the Scottish Parliament represents the real balance of Scottish society much more accurately than our Westminster MPs ever could, and despite all the efforts of the parliament itself to publicise its work and involve citizens in it, voter involvement continues to decline; the turnout at the decisive Scottish election of 2007 was barely more than 50%, and in 2003 the figure was even lower. The reputation of the Scottish Parliament was not helped, of course, by the long-running debacle surrounding the construction of its elaborate new home at Holyrood, a building which still divides opinion; and MSPs themselves, scarred by their atrocious press, showed increasing signs of retreating into a psychological bunker, and excluding all those who were not trusted party-political loyalists.

And that is perhaps one reason why, of all the hopes that surrounded the setting up of the parliament, the hope for a more formal and enduring partnership between parliament, government and Scottish civil society, as enshrined in umbrella organisations like the Constitutional Convention and the Scottish Civic Forum, has proved to be the most forlorn. In one sense, this hope was always doomed to disappointment, because of the nature of civil society itself, which tends to organise as a single movement in times of crisis, but then – quite reasonably – to fragment again into a series of single-issue organisations and lobbying groups when politics returns to normal. In 2005, the Lab-Lib administration led by Jack McConnell withdrew funding from the

Scottish Civic Forum. And apart from some youth initiatives, there has been no further attempt at the European-style public funding of independent civil society forums as active partners in government; indeed MSPs often seem to feel that such bodies simply come between members and their constituents, and try to usurp their special and direct relationship with those they represent.

A Crisis of Democracy?
And in that sense, Scotland's new constitutional settlement remains a hostage to a party-political system which is everywhere in decline, in terms of mass membership and social resonance; but which retains a dominant role in all our formal political institutions. There are aspects of the new Scottish constitutional settlement which successfully modify some of the most negative effects of that decaying party structure; in particular, the accurate reflection of the balance of public opinion in parliament, and the absence of overwhelming parliamentary majorities, represent clear democratic gains achieved through proportional representation. The election, in 2007, of a long-excluded party that has never before held power at national level, and whose activists have been mainstays of civic activity in many parts of Scotland for the last two generations, has also produced a vigorous, if probably transient, sense of a healthy reconnection between formal politics and some parts of civil society.

Yet despite these gains, the new Scottish Parliament – like Westminster, and many other 21st century parliaments – remains trapped between the claims of a declining party system that remains the only path to electoral success; the claims of a civil society which lacks the legitimacy of an elected parliament; and the claims of ordinary, unorganised voters, who feel largely unrepresented by both groups. The campaign for a Scottish Parliament, in the 1990s, was aware of this looming crisis of democracy, and made some brave attempts to tackle it, through a combination of democratic strategies tried and tested elsewhere in Europe, and innovative ideas shaped by technological change.

In the end, its perception of the strength and usefulness of civil society, as a concept and as a sustained representative voice, was slightly exaggerated by the special circumstances of the time; and it can perhaps be accused of applying some late 20th century answers to fast-evolving 21st century questions about power, and how to share it. There is no doubt, though, that the experience of Scotland since 1999 represents a classic study in the interplay between high constitutional ideals on the one hand, and the reality of everyday politics on the other. And wise observers will know that the story is not one about the foolishness of hope and the inevitability of disappointment; but about the area of tension between the two, within which all true political progress is made.

Chapter 10

The Scottish Parliament Electoral System: Can Credibility be Restored?

Nicola McEwen

> *Electoral systems are rarely designed, they are born kicking and screaming into the world out of a messy, incremental compromise between contending factions battling for survival, determined by power politics.*
> (Professor Pippa Norris, Harvard University)

And so it was with the Scottish Parliament electoral system. The introduction of the additional member system (AMS) in Scotland was primarily a political compromise between the Labour Party and the Liberal Democrats, working within the Scottish Constitutional Convention. Although the Liberal Democrats' preference was for the single transferable vote (STV), AMS would at least ensure a degree of proportionality in Scottish parliamentary representation. The Labour Party had most to lose from the introduction of any form of proportional representation (PR) given its disproportionate dominance of constituency seats in first-past-the-post elections. Nonetheless, it was at least reassured that under AMS, the SNP would be unable to form a majority government which could take Scotland to independence without having first won a majority of the popular vote in an election. AMS also had the advantage of maintaining the relationship between elected representatives and the voters in single member constituencies.

AMS is now one of four electoral systems in Scotland, operating alongside the first-past-the-post system in use for Westminster elections, a Scotland-wide list system for elections to the European Parliament and STV in local government elections. Of these, AMS has been the most controversial. Even before the 2007 Scottish Parliament election, when reforms to the system, the ballot paper and its operation alongside STV for local government elections contributed to record numbers of rejected ballot papers, the Scottish Parliament's electoral system was the subject of considerable scrutiny. This chapter will consider the features of the electoral system and the controversies surrounding its reform and operation in 2007, and will question whether its credibility can be recovered in future Scottish parliamentary elections.

The Features of the Scottish Parliament Electoral System
Scotland's additional member system is a form of mixed member proportional (MMP) system, so-called because it combines the election of local constituency

candidates with a vote for a party. Germany was the only example of a mixed member system until the 1990s, but there has been a rapid explosion of this type of system ever since. Commonly, it involves voters casting two votes, one for a local constituency representative and one for a political party. In the constituency vote, the candidate with the most votes wins (as in first-past-the-post). In mixed member proportional systems the party vote is then used to calculate the share of seats each party should have, and the remaining seats are then distributed accordingly. So, in deciding the outcome of an election under MMP, the party vote is the most important.

The German model was the key inspiration for the Scottish Parliament's electoral system in its original form, most notably in the adoption of regional lists instead of the national lists common in other MMP systems. Some of the terminology used to describe the German system also influenced the Scottish model. Although there is only one ballot paper in Germany, the constituency vote is on the left and is called the 'primary vote' (*erststimme*), while the list vote is on the right and is called the 'secondary vote' (*zweitstimme*). In Scotland, constituency and list votes were cast using separate ballot papers in 1999 and 2003, but the constituency vote was commonly referred to as the 'first vote' and the party list vote as the 'second vote'.

However, there are several features particular to the Scottish system which limit the extent to which the list vote can fully compensate for the disproportional outcome of the constituency vote. First, the ratio of constituency to list seats (57% to 43%) is less than the 50:50 ratio of the German system, and leaves us with fewer compensatory list seats to allocate. Second, the counting method used to distribute seats in Scotland (d'Hondt) is generally considered to be the least proportional. Third, a party might win more constituency seats than its share of the regional list vote suggests it should have overall. In Germany (and New Zealand), a party can keep these extra, or 'overhang', seats and the size of the parliament is temporarily enlarged to accommodate them. In Scotland, by contrast, the number of MSPs is fixed at 129, and if one party wins overhang seats in the constituency contest, the other parties receive fewer seats than their share of the list vote entitles them. Fourth, whereas in most MMP systems, only registered political parties can present themselves for election on the list, the Scottish model also allows for the nomination of independent candidates on the regional list. This is highly unusual and runs against the logic of an MMP system, where the main purpose of the list is to compensate for the disproportionality of the first-past-the-post constituency election.

Grasping that the party list vote is designed to compensate for the disproportionality of the constituency vote, and ultimately to determine the share of seats each party holds in parliament, is central to understanding MMP. Yet, this has been little understood by the public and barely appreciated by politicians. A knowledge quiz conducted as part of the 2003 Scottish Social

Attitudes survey revealed that less than one in four respondents understood the purpose and significance of the party list vote, while many thought that the 'second vote' was a second preference. For many politicians, meanwhile, especially within the Labour Party, AMS was an extension of the Westminster electoral system. It retained the single-member constituency representation of the Westminster system, originally using the same constituency boundaries, and PR list members were 'added on'. The lack of understanding of the system may reflect the manner in which the system was introduced in Scotland. Although PR had been discussed and debated in the UK, especially in the late 1980s and early 1990s during Labour's long period of opposition, it was at best a side issue in the politics of home rule. The electoral system, whose detailed proposals emerged from a sub-committee of the Scottish Constitutional Convention, was not chosen because all concerned recognised its superior qualities among the array of electoral systems available. Rather, it was a compromise which, for PR enthusiasts, was the best they could hope for, while for the less enthusiastic, it provided the necessary concession to limited proportionality without losing the traditions of local constituency representation.

Reforming the System
AMS has had its critics since its inception, but two developments prompted the review and subsequent reform of the system in advance of the 2007 election. First, the reduction in the number of Scottish MPs from 72 to 59 meant that the boundaries of Westminster and Scottish parliamentary constituencies were no longer coterminous. Second, the Scottish Parliament passed legislation to introduce STV in local government elections and, as a result, from 2007, Scottish voters would have to deal with four different voting systems when choosing their elected representatives. Under pressure from its own back-benches, the UK government set up the independent Commission on Boundary Differences and Voting Systems (the Arbuthnott Commission), reporting to the secretary of state for Scotland and the First Minister. As part of its remit, the Commission was asked to determine whether these two developments merited a change to the method of voting in Scottish parliamentary elections.

Few of the key political players responding to the Commission's consultation defended AMS in its original form. The SNP and the Liberal Democrats reiterated their long-standing commitment to STV for all elections. The Conservatives and the Labour Party supported retention of AMS (rather grudgingly – both stated their preference for first-past-the-post but accepted that the Commission had to respect the degree of proportionality enshrined in the devolution settlement), but recommended reforms. The Conservatives sought coterminous Westminster and Holyrood boundaries and tentatively supported replacing the two-vote system with a single vote. The Labour Party was also supportive of a single vote system, based on the constituency vote, claiming a lack of understanding among the electorate of the role and purpose of the regional list vote. Labour was also critical of the role, workload and conduct of regional list MSPs, pointing to a 'tendency amongst some list MSPs to cherry pick issues and campaigns for their own political profile and for party purposes rather than in the interests of the constituents they represent'. Labour was critical, too, of the principle of allowing candidates to stand for election simultaneously in the constituencies and on the regional list (dual candidacy), arguing that: 'A situation where in some cases all the candidates who stand in a constituency are then elected from the list has the potential to create a class of MSP who becomes immune to public opinion and effectively cannot be voted out of office.'

The Arbuthnott Commission made a broad range of recommendations in relation to boundaries, representation and the voting system, but two key sets of recommendations bear mention for the subsequent influence they would have. First, and perhaps most influentially, the Commission resisted pressure to introduce reforms to the system that it felt would reduce voter choice and weaken the status of those elected via the regional lists. These included the call to ban dual candidacy and to reduce the number of votes electors have from two to one. This made it more difficult for the Scotland Office to consider following the reform of MMP in Wales set out in the Government of Wales Act 2006 which forced candidates to choose to stand in either the constituency or on the list.

Second, motivated by concerns at the extent of voter confusion over the purpose of electing members on the list, and in particular by survey evidence of a decline in voter understanding of the system between 1999 and 2003, the Commission recommended changing the terms with which the system was described and presented to the electorate. In this regard, the Commission was inspired by the New Zealand model, which uses the term 'mixed member proportional system', provides clear and simple guidance to electors on the purpose of the two votes, and gives paramountcy to the party vote on a single ballot paper. Commending the New Zealand ballot paper, the Arbuthnott Commission recommended 'redesigning the ballot papers to reflect more accurately the way mixed member systems work and to counter perceptions that the regional vote is less important. In mixed member systems, it is the list vote, not the constituency one, which is key to deciding the overall share of seats in the parliament and the election of the government.'

Beyond its commendation of the New Zealand ballot paper, the Commission did not make any specific suggestions of how a revised Scottish ballot paper might look. Indeed, a weakness of its proposals was the lack of consideration of the challenges involved in applying this aspect of the New Zealand model to the Scottish context. For example, the Commission did not give serious consideration to the practice in New Zealand – as in most other mixed member proportional systems – of allowing only registered political parties to stand on the party list vote, and it rejected a proposal to replace regional lists with a national list (as used in New Zealand). This influenced the terminology it recommended: whereas in New Zealand, voters are asked to cast a 'party vote', in Scotland, the Commission suggested they be asked to cast a 'regional vote'. These particular features add a layer of complexity to the Scottish model which is absent from the New Zealand system. As a result, it is much more difficult in the Scottish case to achieve the clarity of the descriptions and explanations on the New Zealand ballot paper and other voter information material.

The Commission's recommendation to change the way the system was presented to voters was partially adopted by the Scotland Office in the redesigned ballot papers presented to voters in 2007. In the event, the instructions to voters on the Scottish ballot papers neither had the clarity of the New Zealand example, nor were they backed by clear explanations as to the purpose of each vote. In addition, voters were asked to digest these changes to the Scottish Parliament electoral system while simultaneously adapting to a wholly new preferential voting system for local government. The subsequent election was to become one of the darkest days in the life of the new Scottish democracy.

What Went Wrong in 2007?
The 2007 elections to the Scottish Parliament produced just under 3% of rejected regional votes and just over 4% of rejected constituency votes. This was substantially higher than in the previous two elections. In the aftermath of the election, the Electoral Commission set up an independent inquiry, headed by Canadian elections expert Ron Gould, to examine the cause of such a high rate of rejected ballots (as well as other administrative and technical problems evident on election day). The Gould Report criticised the lack of research that went into the design of the ballot papers, the political micro-management over the details of the design, and administrative delays in finalising the ballot papers. Above all else, though, it claimed to have strong evidence that 'combining the Scottish parliamentary ballot papers onto one sheet was primarily responsible for the high level of rejected ballot papers'. But why should a practice common in other mixed member systems have created such a problem in Scotland?

It is difficult to isolate the effect of the combined ballot paper from the many other innovations and problems evident on election day. However, there are at least three possible explanations as to why the ballot paper may have created problems in Scotland that have not been evident in other MMP systems. First, coupling the Scottish parliamentary election with its revised ballot paper to a local government election conducted for the first time under STV increased the complexity involved in the task of voting. This may also have made it more difficult for election officials to ensure that the voting procedures *for both elections* were sufficiently understood. Second, not only was the research that led to the *particular* design of the combined ballot papers inadequate, based merely on a small scale focus group study of 100 participants, but the chosen design was not the one which that research suggested voters preferred. Notably absent from the chosen design was any explanation as to the purpose of each vote; as discussed above, such explanations were the principal reason behind the Arbuthnott Commission's commendation of the New Zealand ballot paper. Further, in Glasgow and Lothians, instructions were abbreviated and the directional arrows indicating where to vote were deleted to accommodate the large number of parties and independent candidates (23 in each case) who stood on these regional lists. There is strong evidence to suggest that these alterations at least partially accounted for the higher than average incidence of rejected ballots in these regions. Third, unusually for an MMP system, the Scottish system permits independent candidates to stand alongside parties in the regional list vote. This, along with the practice adopted by some parties of using a named individual instead of their registered party name (e.g. 'Alex Salmond for First Minister') may have led some voters to confuse the regional and constituency contests, and see the constituency vote on the right as a continuation of the regional vote on the left.

The Gould Report made several recommendations intended to minimise the number of rejected ballots in the future, including reverting to two separate ballot papers for the regional and constituency vote, having parties listed on the regional ballot paper by their registered name (rather than a slogan or named individual), and decoupling local government and Scottish parliamentary elections. The UK and Scottish governments have accepted these recommendations.

Conclusion: Can the Credibility of the System be Restored?
Whether the credibility of the voting system is restored will largely depend on voters' perceptions of, and trust in, the political process. The anticipated changes to the planning and conduct of the election should help to avoid a repeat of the rejected ballots debacle of 2007, and we can reasonably expect the number of votes considered 'invalid' to return to the levels seen in 1999 and 2003. For a vote to be truly valid, however, it should accurately reflect the genuine preferences of the voter. An elector who falsely believes that the list vote is a second preference, or who fails to appreciate its importance in determining the outcome of the election, may cast votes which are formally counted as valid, but if these votes do not reflect their true preferences, a higher standard of validity will continue to elude us. It is worth remembering that the original motivation for revising the ballot paper was to address voter misunderstanding of the system, and in particular of the purpose and importance of the list vote. If the reversion to two ballot papers is accompanied by a return to the language of 'first' and 'second' votes to describe the constituency and regional list votes respectively, it will leave the original problem unresolved.

Thomas Lundberg has suggested that at the core of this 'ballot paper problem'…'lies a deeper problem: understanding that MMP is a form of proportional representation'.[1] Central to the successful functioning of the system is an understanding that list votes are intended to correct the disproportionality of the constituency vote and that a party's share of parliamentary seats should approximate its share of list votes. Some features peculiar to the Scottish system, most notably the lack of any mechanism for dealing with overhang seats, and the inclusion of independent candidates on the regional list, run counter to this technical purpose of mixed member proportional systems. I am not suggesting that we adopt the New Zealand and German practice of temporarily increasing the size of the parliament to accommodate overhang seats; political or popular appetite for such a move seems unlikely. Nor am I suggesting that the inclusion of independents on the list is a weakness of the Scottish system; to date, only one MSP has stood *and* been elected as an independent regional list member (Margo MacDonald, Lothians list), but few would doubt that her contribution to the life of the parliament has been substantial. Rather, these features add to the challenge facing election officials tasked with the responsibility of informing the public of how the system works and how their votes contribute to the election of a government. Without better and more effective communication, the anticipated achievement in reducing the number of formally invalid votes may mask a degree of confusion over the role and purpose of both votes. If this confusion affects *how* people vote – and especially if it results in some voters choosing their second preference party or candidate because they are under the false impression that this is what they are supposed to do – then the voting system will continue to tarnish the democratic process in Scotland.

[1] T.C. Lundberg (2008), 'An opposing view of Scotland's ballot paper problem: Arbuthnott and the Government had the right idea?', *The Political Quarterly*, Vol.79, No.4, pp. 569-77.

Chapter 11

New Parliament, New Elections

James Mitchell and Robert Johns

Introduction
The advent of devolution meant the advent of Scottish parliamentary elections. Previously, the only Scottish-wide elections – apart from local council elections – had been UK general elections. Now, after three elections to the Scottish Parliament, we can begin to draw tentative conclusions about voting patterns in this new arena. The natural focus of comparison is with Scottish voters' behaviour in UK general elections. However, there are three important differences between the two contexts which need to be borne in mind when making such comparisons. First, as discussed in greater detail by Nicola McEwen in Chapter 10, Scottish Parliament elections are held under a new more proportional representation electoral system. The Additional Member System (AMS) not only gives electors two votes – one for a candidate in their constituency, the other for a party list in their electoral region – but also affords smaller parties a far better chance of gaining seats than in the first-past-the-post (FPTP) system used for Westminster elections. Second, Scottish parties – notably the SNP – are in a much stronger position in elections to the devolved parliament, since they can be key players at Holyrood yet will inevitably be hopelessly outnumbered at Westminster. Third, the nature of devolution is such that a different set of issues and concerns are at stake in Scottish Parliament elections compared with UK general elections. Related, the nature of devolution – especially in fiscal and macroeconomic terms – means that Scottish Parliament elections may be seen overall as less important.

This final point leads to the distinction made by the German political scientists Karlheinz Reif and Hermann Schmitt between first- and second-order elections.[1] By (their) definition, each country has only one first-order election: the 'general' election to its dominant national legislative chamber. All other elections – municipal, regional, upper house, European – are second-order. The crux of Reif and Schmitt's argument is that, because voters perceive less at stake in these second-order elections, their decisions are instead driven by factors inherent in the more important first-order arena. In particular, voters use the opportunity to have a mid-term say on the performance of the national government, which typically results in a poor performance for parties in office. Second-order elections also tend to see greater support for small parties, such as environmental or extreme right parties. Voters are more reluctant

---

[1] K. Reif & H. Schmitt (1980), 'Nine Second-Order National Elections. A Conceptual Framework for the Analysis of European Election Results', *European Journal of Political Research*, 8, pp. 3-44.

to support such parties in first-order elections when, with more at stake, the opportunity cost of such a protest vote is higher. All this assumes that voters have turned out at all, which they are less inclined to do in second-order elections since there is less at stake.

There is good reason to doubt that Scottish Parliament elections are second-order contests as described above. Holyrood's powers comfortably exceed those of local councils or the European Parliament. Moreover, some voters may regard Scottish Parliament elections as more important than UK general elections, perhaps because they give highest priority to devolved issues like education and health, or perhaps because a strong Scottish identity leads some electors to see elections to the Scottish Parliament as the real 'national' election. This highlights the key point that voters differ in their perceptions of, and hence their decision-making in, different elections. Another illustration of the same point is the fact that some voters, having strong attachments to a particular party, are likely to vote for that party in both Scottish Parliament and UK general elections regardless of the electoral system, the relative importance of the two elections, or indeed anything else. These caveats notwithstanding, Reif and Schmitt's three characteristics of second-order elections – lower turnout, stronger showing for small parties, weaker showing by governing parties – are useful for structuring our comparison of voting patterns in Scottish Parliament and UK general elections.

Turnout

In Table 1 we present Scottish turnout percentages in three types of election – to the UK, Scottish and European Parliaments – since 1997. There are three points to note. First, turnout in Scottish elections has consistently been lower than in the preceding UK general election. Second, however, that gap is narrowing – it was 12.3 points between 1997 and 1999, 8.4 between 2001 and 2003 and 6.9 between 2005 and 2007. Third, turnout in Scottish Parliament elections is much greater than in European Parliament elections. (We use European elections rather than local council elections for comparison because council elections have been held on the same day as Scottish Parliament elections since 1999.) The implication is that Scottish Parliament elections more closely resemble first- than second-order elections, and seem to be getting 'more first-order' over time. This is consistent with the notion that, as the devolved institutions become more embedded and more influential, voters see more at stake and are readier to turn out in Scottish Parliament elections. On the other hand, the narrowing of the turnout gap between UK general and Scottish Parliament elections may simply reflect a specific feature of the 2007 election, namely the widespread anticipation of a close contest between Labour and the SNP, rather than a longer-term trend. Further elections – in both arenas – are needed to clarify this point.

Table 1: Scottish Turnout (%) in UK General, Scottish Parliament and European Elections, 1997–2007

	UK General	Scottish Parliament	European Parliament
May 1997	71.3		
May 1999		59.0	
June 1999			24.7
June 2001	58.1		
May 2003		49.7	
June 2004			30.6
May 2005	60.8		
May 2007		53.9	

Party Vote Shares

The other two features of second-order elections concern party vote shares, and here things are complicated by the different electoral systems used at Holyrood and Westminster. For a variety of reasons discussed by Joyce McMillan in Chapter 9, supporters of devolution were keen that the Scottish Parliament should be 'more representative' than an FPTP system would allow. The choice of a more proportional system ensured that seat allocations better reflected Scotland's multi-party politics, both the presence of an additional main party and the unusually strong showing of the left. However, electoral systems have not only a 'mechanical' impact – the way in which vote shares are translated into seat shares – but also a 'psychological' impact on voters. In particular, because proportional systems give smaller parties a greater chance of winning seats, they also give voters more incentive to choose such parties. This is well illustrated when we consider regional list voting in Scottish Parliament elections (as shown in the left-hand panel of Table 2). The 'others' (minor parties and independent candidates) have taken a substantial proportion of the list vote in all three elections. Their performance peaked in 2003, a vote share of 22% resulting in the election of 15 MSPs from outside the main four parties.

Table 2: Vote Shares in UK General and Scottish Parliament Elections, 1997–2007

	% List Votes			% Constituency Votes (cf. UK General)					
	1999	2003	2007	1997	1999	2001	2003	2005	2007
Labour	34	29	29	46	39	44	35	40	32
SNP	27	21	31	22	29	20	24	18	33
Conservative	15	16	14	17	16	16	17	16	17
Lib Dem	12	12	11	13	14	16	15	23	16
Others	12	22	15	2	3	4	9	4	2

On a second-order reading, these strong showings by smaller parties reflect voters freed by the relative unimportance of the election to cast an experimental or rebellious ballot. However, comparing list and constituency voting implicates the electoral system rather than the status of the election. Aside from a spike in 2003, the minor parties typically claim between just two and four percent of constituency votes in either Scottish Parliament or UK general elections. The particularly low percentage in 2007 is doubtless due partly to the sharp decline in the number of 'other' candidates contesting constituencies. Yet this 'supply-side constraint' was itself probably motivated by a lack of demand – it reflects the minor parties' struggle to win significant constituency votes.

The third feature of voting in second-order elections is a poor showing by parties in office at the national or first-order level. Comparing constituency vote shares in Scottish Parliament and UK general elections, we can see that Labour (which formed the UK government throughout the first 10 years after devolution) lost support at each Scottish Parliament election as compared with the previous UK general election (Table 2). Yet the difference is not huge – averaging at around seven percentage points – and is certainly narrower than with, say, European elections, in which incumbents at Westminster tend to suffer acutely. Moreover, Labour's lost support is not spread among the other parties in the way that might be expected of a protest vote, but instead seems to go largely to the SNP. This looks more like an 'arena effect' than a second-order effect. One reason for an arena effect was noted above: SNP votes might be thought wasted, and will certainly be swamped, in a UK general election, whereas they carry much more weight in a Scottish Parliament contest. A slightly different reason was suggested by Lindsay Paterson and his colleagues on the basis of their study of the 1999 election in which 'voters revealed that what they are looking for in a Scottish election are parties that are willing to use the devolved institutions to promote Scotland's interests'. We drew a parallel conclusion about the 2007 election from the SNP's considerable advantage over Labour in terms of the perceived commitment to Scottish interests.

Similar conclusions are suggested by survey data from 2007 asking voters whether and how they would have voted had it been a UK general election rather than a Scottish Parliament election. The SNP's one-point lead in the constituency vote would have been a six-point deficit in a UK general election. However, when those who would have voted differently in a Westminster contest were asked why, just 22% reported that they were 'using the Scottish Parliament elections to send a message to London'. More common than this second-order motivation were two reasons indicating an arena effect: 'no single party has the best policies for both Scotland and Britain' (33%) and 'I really prefer a party that has no chance of forming the Westminster government' (28%). This latter reason was cited by fully 55% of those who reported a Scottish Parliament vote intention for the SNP. Again, then, the differences in voting patterns have less to do with the relative importance of elections to the UK and Scottish Parliaments and more to do with the different opportunities for parties, and the different considerations in voters' minds, in the two arenas.

The Promiscuous Scottish Electorate

As Gilbert and Sullivan put it in the 19th century: 'Every little boy and girl/ That's born into this world alive/ Is either a little liberal/ Or a little conservative.' Even as late as the 1960s, most electors aligned themselves with one of the two main British parties. However, both the proportion of voters reporting a partisan loyalty and the average strength of such loyalties have long been in decline. These trends, often summarised as 'partisan dealignment', are not confined to Scotland – or for that matter to Britain – but they have had particular impact on Scottish politics since 1999 because the additional level of elections and the two-vote electoral system have given voters ample opportunity to switch between parties. Put another way, dealignment created a potentially promiscuous electorate, and the electoral institutions of devolution tend to encourage such promiscuity.

So far this chapter has already provided considerable indirect evidence of voters' willingness to switch between parties. The healthy showing of the minor parties in Scottish elections, and in particular their surge in 2003, give an indication that many voters feel no particular loyalty to the older and more established parties. There was an almost equally steep decline in support for the 'others' between 2003 and 2007 while the SNP saw a major upturn in its share of the vote. Vote shares thus vary markedly between different elections to the Scottish Parliament as well as between Scottish Parliament and UK general elections. Such volatility in party support is another feature of a dealigned electorate.

Moreover, aggregate vote shares give only an impression of the total extent of volatility in party choice at the individual level. We mentioned earlier a survey question asking voters at Scottish Parliament elections how they would have voted had the election instead been to Westminster. In 2007, 76% would have opted for the same party in their constituency. The equivalent proportion at the 1999 election was 82%. These figures confirm that a considerable and perhaps a growing number of voters are becoming accustomed to choosing different parties in elections at different levels. Switching between different Scottish Parliament elections is still more common. In 2007, only the SNP was able to retain the support of four in five of its 2003 voters. For Labour and the Conservatives the corresponding proportion was only around two-thirds, and for the Liberal Democrats it was even smaller.

A rather different kind of switching between parties is 'ticket-splitting', voting for different parties on the two ballot papers (or same ballot paper in 2007) at the same election According to the relevant survey data, the proportion of ticket-splitters is on the increase: from 18% in 1999 to 28% in 2003 and then up to 30% in 2007. This trend is driven largely by an increase in splitting between major and minor parties. In 2003 this was due to the impressive showing by the minor parties; in 2007 it had more to do with the fact that very few minor parties contested constituency seats and so almost all of those who supported a minor party (or an independent) on the list were thus forced into ticket-splitting (or leaving the constituency vote blank). That said, a far from trivial proportion (11%) of voters in 2007 voted for two different major parties, and a good deal of ticket-splitting was between parties supposed to be sworn enemies. Overall, the clear impression is again one of voters increasingly embracing the opportunity to switch between parties.

Conclusions

The underlying question for this chapter concerns whether voting patterns in Scottish Parliament elections are in some sense new and distinct from those in UK general elections. That question has often been examined using the lens of second-order elections. But there is a paradox inherent in that approach. The defining characteristic of second-order elections is that the results diverge – small parties doing better, governing parties doing worse – from those that would be expected in a first-order election. Yet it would be odd to pursue that logic and to conclude that Scottish elections would be purely first-order if the results precisely matched those of Westminster elections. Certainly this was not the aim at the inception of devolution. Scottish Parliament elections were supposed to be different from UK general elections, not because they would be seen as less important, but because they would reflect the Scottish party system and the particular needs and preferences of Scottish voters.

By that yardstick we can deliver a fairly optimistic verdict. On the negative side, turnout is lower than in UK general elections and the evidence suggests that this is because of a gap in the perceived influence of the two arenas. However, the differences in vote shares between Scottish Parliament and Westminster elections give the former a distinctly Scottish (as opposed to a second-order) flavour. The more proportional electoral system gives expression to the complexity of party politics and ensures a parliament more representative of the voters' partisan preferences. Equally, the comparative advantage for the SNP over Labour in Scottish Parliament elections – and indeed the result in 2007 – reflect specifically Scottish factors, principally the SNP's greater relevance at Holyrood and its perceived willingness to use the new parliament to fight for Scottish interests.

It is conceivable – indeed almost certain – that Scottish elections are not in any sense second-order for some voters. Who these voters are and whether this is a growing or shrinking part of the electorate needs to be explored.

Care has to be taken in making any general statements about how the Scottish electorate, consisting of individual voters and not socially coherent amalgams, as often implied in much commentary, behaves. Crucially, we stress that the electorate is not static, that any findings or assumptions may change over time and that the electorate is not a 'single actor' but a vast and changing collection of individual citizens.

Chapter 12

Do Devolved Elections Work?

John Curtice

There were of course many motivations behind the demand for a devolved Scottish Parliament. But one argument commonly espoused by devolution's advocates was that it would enhance the quality of Scotland's democracy. No longer would it be possible for an unpopular government, such as the Conservative government of 1979-97, to foist on Scotland unpopular policies, such as the poll tax, and be immune to the adverse judgement of Scottish voters because it could secure election and re-election on the basis of votes cast in England. Now those who aspired to be responsible for Scotland's domestic affairs would have to demonstrate that their policy proposals had the support of the country's voters and that their performance in office met with voters' approval.

Such an aspiration seemed a perfectly reasonable one. In a liberal democracy elections are often regarded as a mechanism that, first, ensures the views of those who are responsible for passing laws are representative of the society in which those laws apply and, second, guarantees that the government of a country is accountable to the people it is supposed to serve. Yet it was also an aspiration whose realisation depended on the behaviour of Scotland's voters. An election has little chance of producing a parliament whose views are representative of the distribution of opinion in society unless voters take account of the policy proposals of the parties in deciding how to vote. Equally, an election will prove a poor mechanism for holding governments to account if voters do not decide how to vote on the basis of how well or badly they think the incumbent government has performed.

How far voters behave in this way in any election is regularly and sometimes fiercely debated. But there are particular reasons to wonder whether they are likely to do so in a devolved election. Once responsibility for government is divided between two or more tiers or levels, it can become difficult for voters to decide who is responsible for a particular outcome. Say, for example, someone is unhappy with the state of the health service in Scotland. Should they blame the Scottish government on the grounds it is responsible for the management of the NHS north of the border, or should they consider the UK government responsible because it decides the overall budget within which the Scottish government has to operate? Meanwhile, thanks to the use of proportional representation in Scottish Parliament elections, coalition governments are quite likely, as proved to be the case between 1999 and

2007. So even if voters believe the Scottish government should be blamed, they might still be left wondering which party in particular deserves to have opprobrium heaped upon it.

Equally the behaviour of voters in an election may depend on how important they consider the body being elected to be. If they regard it as relatively unimportant they might feel their vote is better used to express their views about something more important. This, for example, is what often seems to happen in elections to the European Parliament. Few voters seem to decide how to vote in these contests on the basis of the issues confronting Europe as a whole; many appear to regard them instead as a chance to express an opinion about the performance of their country's incumbent state-level government. So if voters in Scotland were to be of the view that their devolved government was less powerful than its counterpart in London, they might use Scottish Parliament elections to express their views about the performance and policies of the UK government rather than their judgement of the position at Holyrood.

In this chapter we assess whether voters in Scotland have indeed behaved in Scottish Parliament elections in accordance with the expectations of the architects of devolution. Do voters vote in devolved elections on the basis of the policy issues that lie within the competence of the Scottish Parliament and on which the parties are divided? Or are they in fact more likely to vote on the basis of those issues within Westminster's competence that are currently the subject of controversy? Equally, do voters take into account how well or badly they believe the incumbent Scottish administration has performed over the last four years? Or are Scottish elections more likely to be regarded as an opportunity to send a protest note to Westminster? We address these questions by focusing on the 2003 and 2007 Scottish Parliament elections, the two contests held to date at which there was an incumbent Scottish administration with a record to defend. Our evidence comes from the Scottish Social Attitudes survey which has been charting the reaction of the Scottish public to devolution on an annual basis since 1999.

Representation
We consider first how far the way in which people vote in Scottish Parliament elections reflects their views about the desirable direction of policy in respect of those issues that it falls within Holyrood's competence to decide. Table 1 summarises the distribution of opinion within Scotland on some of the issues that were widely discussed at the time of the 2003 and 2007 Scottish elections. It includes both issues such as the introduction of free bus passes for those aged 60 and over and the abolition of prescription charges that lay within the power of Holyrood to determine (devolved issues) and those, such as the decision in 2003 to invade Iraq, that are still determined by Westminster (reserved issues).

Table 1: Policy Preferences in Scotland, 2003 and 2007		
	Agree (%)	Disagree (%)
2003		
Cut business taxes to strengthen Scotland's economy	60	16
Free bus passes to all over 60 even though most could afford to pay	74	18
Britain was wrong to go to war with Iraq	42	40
2007		
Cut business taxes to strengthen Scotland's economy	57	14
Introduce local income tax[a]	83	12
No student should have to pay fees[b]	28	70
Abolish all prescription charges	44	42
Britain was wrong to go to war with Iraq	66	18
Agree with British government decision to renew Trident	39	42

Notes: [a] Question asked respondents whether it was better for local taxation to be based on people's income or on the value of their property. Those who said income are classified as 'agree', while those who said property are classified as 'disagree'.

[b] Question asked respondents to choose between all students paying tuition costs, some paying costs or none at all paying costs. Those giving one of the first two answers are classified as 'disagree'.

The table perhaps contains one or two surprises. Although the decision to abolish upfront university tuition fees is often regarded as one of the iconic differences in public policy north and south of the border brought about by devolution, public opinion in Scotland is not necessarily opposed to tuition fees. The current SNP government's decision to imitate the policy of the Welsh Assembly government of abolishing all prescription charges, thereby opening up another policy difference with England, divides public opinion down the middle. And while by 2007 the Iraq war was clearly unpopular, shortly after the invasion in 2003 it still commanded considerable support.

However, what interests us is whether people's views were reflected in the way in which they voted. All of the policies in Table 1 were ones that were promoted by one or more parties at the time of the 2003 or 2007 election and opposed (or at least not backed) by others. For example, in both 2003 and 2007, cutting business taxes (by reducing business rates) was regarded as a priority by both the SNP and the Conservatives, but was not backed by any of the other parties. So if people's views on that subject were reflected in their votes then those who agreed with cutting business taxes should have been particularly likely to have voted in 2003 and 2007 for either the Conservatives or the SNP, while those who disagreed should have voted for one of the other parties.

Table 2 indicates how far this happened in practice. It shows what proportion of those who supported or opposed a particular policy position voted for a party whose views were in accordance with that position. If policy preference matched party choice perfectly, then all of the entries in the table would be 100%. That of course is unrealistic, but if people's views on an issue are reflected at all in how they vote then the figure (for both supporters and opponents) should be well above 50% (a figure that could occur even if voters were voting at random). However, for the most part the figures for the devolved issues in the first half of the table are little more than 50%. Only in the case of cutting business taxes – and then only in 2007 – is there some suggestion of an alignment between views and votes. In contrast, if we look at the reserved issues in the second half of the table then typically around three-fifths or so of people cast a vote that reflected their views on that issue.

Table 2: Policy Preferences and Vote Choice in Scotland, 2003 and 2007		
	Vote for party consistent with position amongst those who:	
	Support policy (%)	Oppose policy (%)
Devolved Issues		
2003		
Cut business taxes to strengthen Scotland's economy	45	57
Free bus passes to all over 60 even though most could afford to pay	50	53
2007		
Cut business taxes to strengthen Scotland's economy	59	64
Introduce local income tax	49	57
No student should have to pay fees	49	52
Abolish all prescription charges	47	49
Reserved Issues		
2003		
Britain was wrong to go to war with Iraq	52	64
2007		
Britain was wrong to go to war with Iraq	58	64
Agree with British government decision to renew Trident	61	62

Accountability

But did voters, nevertheless, use Scottish Parliament elections to hold the administration in Edinburgh to account? Or were they more likely to use the occasion to send a protest note to Westminster? Table 3 shows the response people gave in 2007 when they were asked to say, first, how good a job of running Britain the UK Labour government had done in recent years and, second, how good a job of running Scotland Labour ministers in the Scottish executive had done. In both cases more people felt Labour had done a good job than believed it had performed badly, though its record at Westminster was regarded a little more favourably than that at Holyrood.

Table 3: Overall Evaluations of Labour's Performance in the UK Government and Scottish Executive, 2007

	Evaluation of Labour's Performance in	
	UK Government	Scottish Executive
	%	%
Very Good	6	2
Fairly Good	43	37
Neither Good Nor Bad	25	33
Fairly Bad	15	15
Very Bad	8	5
Can't Choose	4	8

However, what is crucial for our purposes is whether those who were dissatisfied with Labour's performance were less likely to back the party than those who were satisfied. Table 4 presents the results of one very simple way of examining whether that was the case. It confines its attention to those who reported (in 2007) that they had backed Labour in 2003, and shows what proportion of this group turned out and voted for Labour again in 2007, doing so separately for those who thought Labour had performed well in office and those who did not. If voters' evaluations of Labour's record made a difference to how they voted we should find that those who were dissatisfied with the party's performance were less likely to have supported it again in 2007.

Table 4: Loyalty of Labour Voters by Evaluations of the UK Government and Scottish Executive

% 2003 Labour voters voting Labour in 2007	Evaluation of Labour's record in	
	UK Government	Scottish Executive
Evaluation		
Good	64	62
Not Good	38	49

Evidently that was the case. However, unhappiness with Labour's record at Westminster seems to have been more telling than discontent with its performance in Edinburgh. Those who did not think the UK Labour government had done a good job of running Britain were 26 percentage points less likely to vote for the party again than were those who felt it had done a good job; the equivalent figure in respect of evaluations of the party's performance in Scotland was just 13 points.

Still, it is often argued that elections nowadays have become 'presidentialised'. Perhaps rather than voting on the basis of what they think about the collective performance of governments voters focus instead on what they think of their leaders. So in Table 5 we show how voters responded when they were asked to give Tony Blair a mark out of 10 to show how good a job they thought he had done as Prime Minister, and also what they said when asked to rate Jack McConnell's performance as First Minister in the same way. Tony Blair was evidently the more popular of the two characters, though it seems that most voters felt that Mr McConnell had performed indifferently rather than badly.

Table 5: Evaluations of Tony Blair and Jack McConnell, 2003 and 2007	2003 (%)	2007 (%)
Tony Blair		
Good (7-10 points)	41	39
Middle (4-6)	39	35
Bad (0-3)	18	24
Don't know	2	2
Jack McConnell		
Good (7-10 points)	20	23
Middle (4-6)	48	45
Bad (0-3)	18	22
Don't know	14	10

But did these evaluations make a difference to the way in which people voted? Table 6 approaches this question in the same way as Table 4, showing what proportion of those who voted Labour at the previous election did so again and how this varied according to how well they believed Mr Blair and Mr McConnell had performed. Once again, both evaluations seem to have made a difference. In 2003, however, those who were unhappy with Tony Blair's performance were far less likely to have voted Labour again than were those who felt Jack McConnell had not done well. In 2007, meanwhile, it looks as though evaluations of Mr Blair had as much influence on the loyalty of Labour voters as did perceptions of Mr McConnell.

Table 6: Labour Loyalty by Evaluations of Labour Party Leaders		
	Evaluation of	
	Tony Blair	Jack McConnell
% 1999 Labour voters voting Labour in 2003		
Evaluation		
Good	68	67
Middle	48	57
Bad	6	30
% 2003 Labour voters voting Labour in 2007		
Evaluation		
Good	62	68
Middle	47	49
Bad	35	42

Conclusion

To date at least, devolved elections do not appear to have been particularly effective at ensuring that those who legislate for Scotland have views that are representative of the country or at guaranteeing that those in power in Edinburgh are accountable to the country's voters. Westminster has got in the way. People's attitudes towards reserved issues have been more likely to be reflected in how they vote while voters seem at least as inclined, if not more so, to vote on the basis of the performance of the UK government at Westminster. That, of course, does not necessarily mean that the quality of democracy in Scotland has been damaged by devolution, but some of the anticipated benefits of the constitutional change have certainly proved more elusive than its advocates had anticipated.

Chapter 13

Conundrums and Contradictions: What Scotland Wants

David McCrone

Looking back over the decade of devolution, two things lodge in the memory. The first is the euphoria, driven, in retrospect, by relief that what had taken 20 years had finally come to pass. The second was the sense of reality, or even disappointment, which set in after a year or two, that Scotland had not been instantly transformed by regaining a parliament. The lightning conductor, as it were, was the controversy over the cost of the new parliament building, some £400 million, and the long process it took to settle down. The media in particular, and not simply those who were hostile to Scottish self-government from the outset, found it a long-running story, and the girn about the parliament and its new home did not dissipate until late 2004, when Peter Fraser's Holyrood Inquiry report was published.

Hindsight is, as always, a wonderful thing, and we have the advantage of a long, almost annual, series of high-quality surveys, the Scottish Social Attitudes surveys, run by the National/Scottish Centre for Social Research. These allowed for a more sober assessment as to how well, or badly, devolution and the parliament had done in the eyes of Scots.

What did Scots Want?

So, what, then, did Scots want? First of all, it is important to say that in terms of constitutional preferences, they wanted, above all, a devolved parliament. Only in September 1997, shortly after the referendum when people voted by three to one in favour of devolution did the independence option come top. Strange as it may seem – the first conundrum – having thrown their weight behind devolution, more Scots said they preferred independence to devolution (by 37% to 32%). Thereafter, however, devolution was comfortably ahead of independence by a significant margin, suggesting to some that it had become, in John Smith's phrase, 'the settled will'.

If devolution was designed to see off the independence option, and with it the SNP – as Labour's George Robertson hoped and thought it would – it seems at first glance to have worked. Except, however, that in 2007 the nationalists won the election, albeit as a minority government. The second conundrum is that they did so despite support for independence barely touching 25%, less than half of the support for the devolution option.

How could the SNP have done so well, and its core policy be supported only

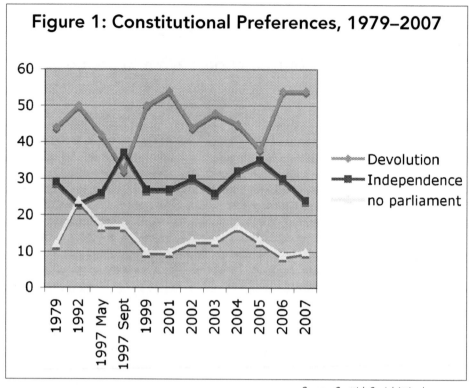

Figure 1: Constitutional Preferences, 1979–2007

Source: Scottish Social Attitudes surveys

by one in four Scots? The long answer is that SNP success in 2007 was due to a number of factors: those who supported independence voting SNP in unprecedented numbers; as did those who wanted a more powerful, albeit devolved, parliament (now becoming known as 'devolution-max'); and those who described themselves as Scottish, not British. Finally, there was the Salmond factor which brought all these together; in other words, leadership mattered. The short answer is that Scots tend not to see elections as a battle between competing constitutional options, reflected in support for different political parties. Rather, the constitutional options should be seen less as categories and more as points on a continuum of self-government. Thus, we find another conundrum, that two-thirds of people throughout the decade wanted the parliament to have more powers than it has (with the exception of the year the parliament began, 1999, when it was 56%).

While in theoretical terms, the Scottish Parliament is a creature of Westminster, it is 'devolved', and could be prorogued should it be so desired, that is not how Scots see it. They are well aware that of the two institutions, Westminster has the most influence over how Scotland is run, but that is a question of 'is', not 'ought'.

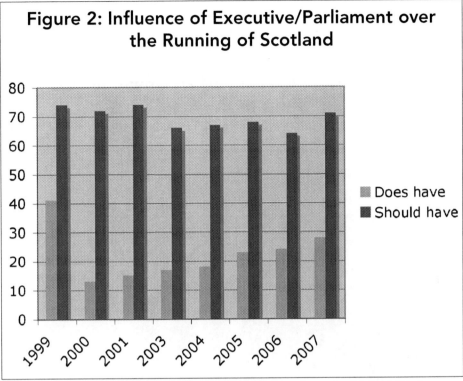

Figure 2: Influence of Executive/Parliament over the Running of Scotland

Legend: Does have / Should have

Source: Scottish Social Attitudes surveys

Only in the heady days of 1999 did a significant proportion, but never a majority, attribute a lot of influence to the Scottish Parliament vis-à-vis the British one. Note two things, however: that by the first year of the parliament, there had been a reality check, and only 13% thought it had most influence over the way Scotland was run; and that this figure has grown year-on-year to 28% by 2007. The most obvious point to draw, however, is the massive disparity between the proportions who think it *does* have the major influence compared with the proportion who think it *should* have, never less than two-thirds of Scots. If the ratio of those who think the Scottish Parliament or executive *should* have the most influence compared with what it is judged to have is around three to one (71% to 28%), the ratio for the UK level of government is one to four (11% to 47%). It is almost, but not quite, a mirror image.

We can see something similar with regard to people's assessment as to how well, or badly, they think the different levels of government listen to people's views. Thus, while Scots are evenly divided as regards how good the Scottish government is at listening to people's views (an equal proportion, 43%, think it is 'good' and 'not good'), it does much better than the UK government, where pessimists outnumber optimists by more than three to one (21% 'good' to 75% 'not good').

The point about trust in Scottish government is reinforced when we look at differential trust levels. More than twice as many are prepared to trust the Scottish level of government compared with the British level.

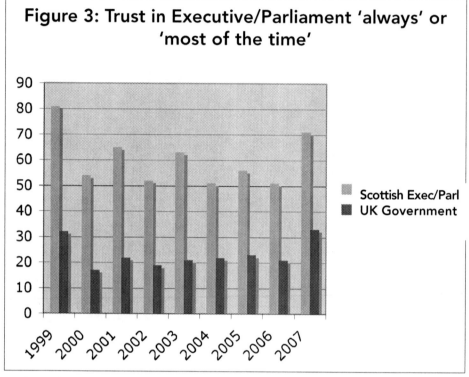

Figure 3: Trust in Executive/Parliament 'always' or 'most of the time'

Source: Scottish Social Attitudes surveys. The question posed was: 'How well do you trust Scottish Executive/ Parliament [UK government] to work in Scotland's long-term interest?'

What has been the Parliament's Impact?

Trust and influence aside, what impact do people think the Scottish Parliament has had? The interesting feature of the following graph, which charts the percentage who think that the parliament (a) 'gives ordinary people more say in how Scotland is governed'; and (b) 'gives Scotland a stronger voice in the UK', is the rapid drop from the utopian days of 1999 and 2000, and the rise in optimism in the later years of the decade, with a dip in the middle.

These assessments could, of course, be based on ignorance, or misunderstanding as to what powers the Scottish Parliament actually has vis-à-vis Westminster. Given that elections, whether Scottish or British, seem to be about similar things – health, education, the economy and so on – how well versed are people in the relevant responsibilities of the respective levels of government?

Do people actually know which level of government makes decisions? They seem to. They get it right on health, education and even on defence and foreign

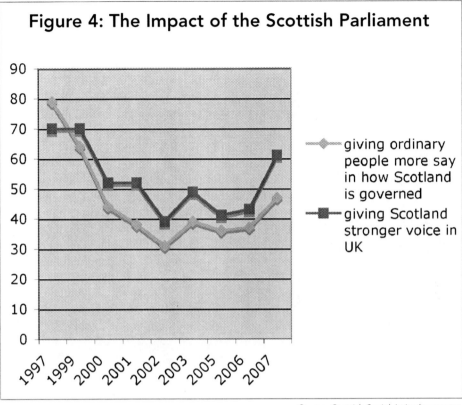

Figure 4: The Impact of the Scottish Parliament

giving ordinary people more say in how Scotland is governed

giving Scotland stronger voice in UK

Source: Scottish Social Attitudes surveys

affairs, while, excusably, misattributing 'welfare' to a Scottish responsibility whereas social security is formally a UK matter. It is nevertheless interesting that Holyrood seems to be a much more salient and important level of government to most people, and that as many as one-third even think it has responsibility for defence and foreign affairs.

It is of course one thing to know what governments are responsible for, and quite another to think they are doing a good job. The Scottish Social Attitudes surveys have asked people over the decade whether they think such services have improved or deteriorated. These assessments show year-on-year variation, with the largest number of people saying they have more or less stayed the same. What is of greater relevance, however, is who they judge to get the credit for improvements and who they blame for deteriorating services.

In the 2006 book *Has Devolution Delivered?*, the authors identified another conundrum. Taking the results for 2003, they showed that the Scottish government got the credit for improvements in services, be they health, education, and even standard of living, whereas the UK government got the blame for deterioration. This was regardless of who actually had responsibility for these services. 2007

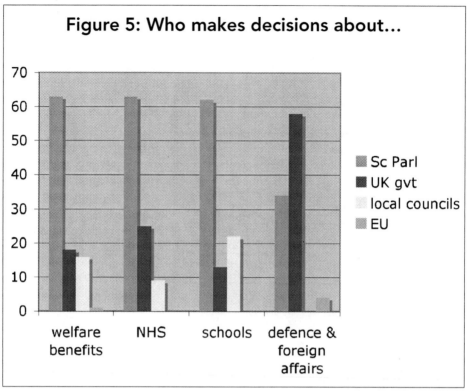

Figure 5: Who makes decisions about...

Source: Scottish Social Attitudes survey, 2007

was a year in which Scots were much more optimistic in their judgements about services, but we find a very similar pattern: optimists credit the Scottish government; pessimists blame the UK one. Thus, on health, people who think services have improved in the past year are more likely to *credit* the Scottish government than the UK one (by 50% to 34%), whereas those who think they have got worse, are more likely to *blame* the UK government than the Scottish one (45% to 14%). Those who think services have remained much the same split 35% to 22% in favour of the UK government, but who gets the credit and blame is the important point.

We find a similar pattern relating to education. Those who think it has improved credit the Scottish government rather than the UK government (by 56% to 21%), whereas for the pessimists, the split is 24% to 46% respectively. In other words, the Scottish level tends to get the credit for improvements, and the British level the blame for deteriorating services. Those who think they have stayed the same split almost equally, 30% to 28%.

Health and education are indubitably 'Scottish government' services. Might it not be that Scots are simply giving credit where it might be constitutionally due? It is not as simple as that as we can see if we do a similar exercise for 'standard of living' and 'the economy', both of which are under the control of Westminster with its powers over taxation. This time, while optimists, those who think things have improved, are marginally more likely to credit Westminster than Holyrood (36% to 32%), they are far more likely to blame deteriorating standards of living on the former than the latter (by 56% to 10%). On the Scottish economy, we even find that those who think it has got stronger in the last 12 months are actually more likely to credit the Scottish government than the UK one (37% to 23%), whereas those who are pessimistic split evenly 27% to 27% (as do those who think there has been no change: 26% to 26%).

What we find, then, is that Scots are more likely to trust the Scottish Parliament to work in the national interest than the British one, and that they give it credit for improvements even where it is not a devolved matter. What, if any, is the relationship between who gets the credit and the blame, and whether or not the parliament should have greater powers? We might expect, for example, that those who think things have got worse and who blame the Scottish government would not want it to have more powers; just as those who credit the UK government for improvements also would not. That is not what we find.

Table 1: Percent Wanting Scottish Parliament to Have More Powers				
	UK Government: worse	UK Government: better	Scottish Govt.: worse	Scottish Govt.: better
NHS	81	58	80	81
Education	76	66	62	76
Standard of living	82	57	63	78
Scottish economy	81	52	60	83

Source: Scottish Social Attitudes survey, 2007

The middle two columns are the crucial ones here. While it is true that those who credit the UK government with improvements (column 2) are somewhat less likely to want more powers for the Scottish Parliament, the figures are comfortably over 50% in every case. Those who think the Scottish government is responsible for deteriorating services (column 3) are even more likely to want it to have more powers. In other words, there is a generic feeling that the Scottish Parliament should have more powers irrespective of who gets the blame and credit, while those who think it has done a good job, and those who think Westminster has not, are more likely to want Holyrood to have more powers.

Funding and Fiscal Autonomy
Throughout the 1990s, the 'Scottish anomaly' – that Scotland got a government

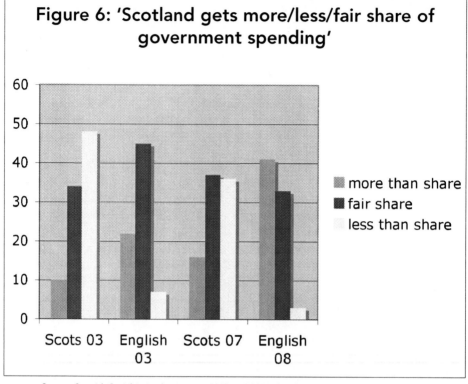

Figure 6: 'Scotland gets more/less/fair share of government spending'

Legend:
- more than share
- fair share
- less than share

Categories: Scots 03, English 03, Scots 07, English 08

Source: Scottish Social Attitudes surveys, 2003 and 2007; British Social Attitudes surveys, 2003 and 2008

at Westminster it did not elect – played an important part in the debate about self-government. Since 1999, however, issues of levels of public spending driven by the Barnett Formula have become more salient, especially in England. How, then, do people in Scotland and England judge Scotland's share of public spending?

While Scots, between 2003 and 2007, have shifted away from the 'less than share' (–12) and towards believing they are getting more than their share (+6), English opinion between 2003 and 2008 has moved far more dramatically towards believing that Scots get more than their share (+19). If we disaggregate this category into 'much more than their share', and 'a little more than their share', it is clear that the shift is towards the more extreme category; 'much more' goes up from 9% in 2003 to 21% in 2008 (+12), whereas the 'little more' category shifts from 13% to 20% (+7). This is in contrast to the early years of devolution (2000–03) where opinion in England changed very little. Perhaps the media and political focus on the Barnett Formula in the second half of the decade is hitting home, and possibly even among the Scots. This is one of few instances where Scottish and English opinion differs substantially, and if anything, is getting more different.

Are Scots looking for a free ride such that they refuse to pay for services in Scotland? It does not seem so:

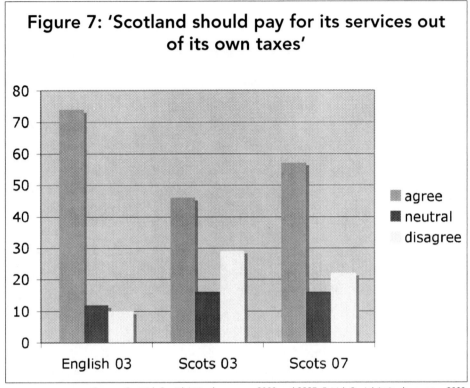

Figure 7: 'Scotland should pay for its services out of its own taxes'

Source: Scottish Social Attitudes survey, 2003 and 2007; British Social Attitudes survey, 2003

'Fiscal autonomy' has its supporters on both sides of the Tweed. We have no data on England in 2008, but given the high proportion (74%) in 2003 who thought Scotland should pay for its own services, it is likely to have strengthened. It is not the case either that Scots think their taxes would be lower. Most – over 50% – expected Scottish taxes to be higher, and only one in 10 that they would be lower.

Independence
Certainly, as far as the founders of devolution were concerned, having a Scottish Parliament within the UK was a way of seeing off the demand for independence: having your cake and eating it, as it were. Is this how Scots see it? Successive surveys have asked:

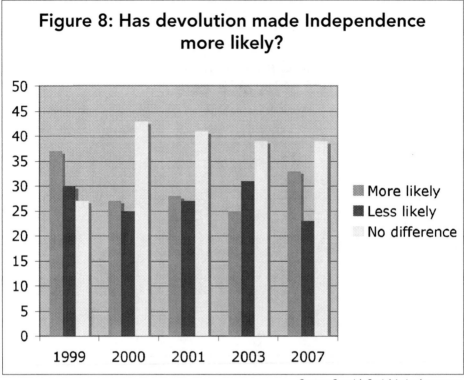

Figure 8: Has devolution made Independence more likely?

Source: Scottish Social Attitudes surveys

So how do people judge this 'slippery slope' or 'thin end of the wedge' argument? By and large, they do not connect devolution to independence, and while there has been a rise in the percentage thinking it will have an effect (from just over a quarter in 2000, to a third in 2007), it is the similarities in public opinion rather than the differences which are more striking. It will be interesting in due course to see what effect, if any, an SNP government will have had on people's perceptions.

And finally: we began this chapter by pointing out that the cost of the Holyrood parliament had become something of a bellwether as regards what people thought of devolution so far. Now that it has disappeared off the political radar, has public opinion changed? What we see is that the outright hostility expressed in agreeing that the parliament at Holyrood should never have been built has waned from 45% in 2003 to just over one-third, and while outright optimists are still few and far between (one in 10), it seems that most people have learned to live with, rather than love, it. Just over half (54%, compared with 46% in 2003) now think that it was needed, but that it cost too much. Politics moves on.

Conclusion

Scottish politics post-devolution continue to intrigue. Conundrums abound. Scots are content with a devolved parliament, but want it to have more powers.

Independence is a minority taste, but they elect a nationalist government. They are critical of Holyrood, but much prefer to give it credit, and allot any blame mainly to Westminster, regardless of the formal division of powers. By and large, they do not see devolution as any kind of slippery slope, or stepping stone, to independence. The person who described devolution as a process rather than an event was more right than he possibly knew at the time.

Chapter 14

New Scottish Parliament, Same Old Interest Group Politics?

Paul Cairney, Darren Halpin and Grant Jordan

New Politics and Unrealistic Expectations

The run-up to devolution was accompanied by an optimism that a new Parliament would institute change in the quality of democracy in Scotland. Pro-devolution reformers did not simply want the repatriation of decision-making to Scotland – they also wanted different decision-making processes. The watchword was a 'new politics' of consensus, participation and deliberation.

For the most optimistic reformers, new political practice was to address two UK tendencies that were portrayed as pathological: governmental dominance of the policy process at the expense of the parliament; and consultation with the 'usual suspects', or the most powerful interest groups, whose close relationships with the government come at the expense of other interests. To leave these unreformed would be to miss the opportunity to exploit the mood of 'civil society' activism in Scotland that in large part drove the devolution agenda. This had emerged, in part, as a response to the 'democratic deficit' (when in 1979–97 the Scottish population voted for a Labour government but received a Conservative government) and a perception of governmental remoteness and antipathy towards the distinctiveness of Scottish policy traditions. The argument was that if the Scottish electorate was being denied democratic control (or at least government responsiveness), then there would be an alternative, more participatory, venue in which to articulate Scottish priorities. A group-oriented politics was also based on criticism of UK politics as an adversarial, non-negotiative system dominated by powerful interests.

But how was this new politics to work? First, there would be a new type of 'participative' democracy, to allow wider involvement in political decisions, and 'deliberative' democracy to produce collective outcomes using reasoned and reasonable arguments among participants affected by policy decisions (this was also 'sold' as a way to solve what were regarded as the confrontational excesses of partisan politics). The main innovations were a petitions process, coordinated by a dedicated parliament committee; and a Scottish Civic Forum (SCF) providing a new venue for involvement and enhanced access for minority groups. The SCF was set up to deliver the participation of hitherto (allegedly) excluded individuals and groups, giving them the chance to engage directly with the Scottish government and parliament. It would include, to some extent, the 'usual suspect' groups who had well-established links to the old system, but in a forum which diluted their influence.

Second, the parliament's committees would take responsibility not only for the scrutiny of government policy, but also the oversight of the relationship between the government and the organisations and individuals that it consulted. The Consultative Steering Group (CSG) recognised that once government policy is presented to the legislature in the form of a 'draft act' it is difficult to change. Therefore, committees would ensure that otherwise-excluded groups would get the chance to influence the policy process at an earlier stage. Committees would then have the chance to reject sections of the bill and/or consult with groups directly if they felt that the government's consultation process had been inadequate. These changes would be supplemented by a process for non-governmental bills in which committees and members (as individuals rather than party hacks) proposed legislation and the lead committee took a central role in the consultation process.

Overall, the hope was for a more pluralist democracy, with the parliament fostering a more transparent consultation process between the government (and parliament itself) and a broader range of groups. Yet, we can detect mixed messages about the centrality of the parliament to this enhanced system. While its committees were central to the petitions process, the SCF represented an alternative venue for group discussion and influence within government. While committees had an enhanced role in the group-government consultation process, there was an assumption that they would only intervene when direct relationships failed. While committees were central to the consultation process on members' bills, the assumption was that the 'government would govern' and that non-executive legislation would be limited.

This lack of a clear 'power-sharing' role reflects a wider ambivalence surrounding the *hopes* for 'new politics' (as a departure from an adversarial system dominated by vested interests) when we recognise the *logic* of government centrality in the consultation process and the *value* of strong parties to political organisation, debate and representative democracy. Further, the mode of delivery of devolution automatically undercut the argument for, and likelihood of, new procedures in two ways. First, the perception of a democratic deficit was substantially remedied when the Scottish population got the Scottish government that it voted for. The complaint of 'English policies for Scottish voters' no longer was valid (for devolved matters at least). Second, the emergence of a stable Labour/Liberal Democrat majority coalition undermined any idea of a shift towards parliament or towards consensus and coalition building between parties inside and outside of government.

From the Rhetoric of New Politics to Business as Usual?
This ambivalence towards new processes and the diffusion of power is reflected

in the actions of the government and parliament. The first significant test of wider participation was the issue dubbed 'Section 28', when widespread objections to the removal of clause 2a (banning the 'promotion' of homosexuality in schools) were dismissed as manufactured public opinion. In other words, devolution reformers assumed that the public would be in tune with their own agendas. When this was not the case, the parliament relied on more traditional forms of (representative) democracy to justify their actions. The SCF did not establish itself as an influential body, in part because it did not succeed in generating broad engagement, and petered out in 2006. While many MSPs describe the petitions process as the 'jewel in our crown' (since it produced considerable activity from individuals and community groups), the government does not consider it a major source of policy innovation.

A more positive picture of a transformed political system can be painted of the post-devolution experience of interest groups. There is a working assumption that hunters 'shoot where the ducks are' – by analogy interest groups organise in ways that reflect changing political decision-making patterns. But contrary to this expectation, the evidence suggests devolution did not lead to the *birth* of many groups (fewer than 20% of groups in Scotland are new). However, groups did more subtly shift their *focus*, with many UK organisations increasing their policy capacity in Scotland and some (such as Unison and the Federation of Small Businesses) devolving greater resources to their Scottish arms.

Interest groups tend to have a positive image of the parliament and government, in part because both are easy to access and willing to consult. Overall, groups claim regular dialogue on substantive issues with policy-makers and judge their lobbying experiences as superior to those enjoyed at UK government level.

Yet, there are three main qualifications to this rosy picture. First, most Scotland -UK comparisons are not reliable because they have a skewed portrayal of UK group-government relations. In fact, many UK-level groups enjoy the same levels of access as their Scottish counterparts. As Jordan and Stevenson suggest, there is a touch of Mandy Rice Davies about group attitudes in Scotland; with many of them having supported the campaign for devolution, they 'would support devolution, wouldn't they?'.

Second, there are signs in Scotland that the traditionally influential groups – the so-called 'usual suspects' – (including local government, the Educational Institute for Scotland and British Medical Association) still dominate consultation with government in their respective areas. Such relationships are based on the 'logic of consultation' – between civil servants and the most interested, active, knowledgeable and representative groups – that drives mutually rewarding links. This logic transcends not only country but also institutional boundaries, with many committees drawing on a similar list of groups when seeking evidence.

Third, after a brief 'honeymoon period' in which groups formed networks, maintained close links with MSPs and responded to consultations outside their usual comfort zone, things returned to 'core business'. Most groups recognised that their main focus should be on the policy issues in which they were engaged directly and with those actors in the government that had dominance in that area. Consequently, the willingness of groups to maintain close links with the parliament diminished. This is indicated by a survey undertaken by Darren Halpin and Iain MacLeod which asked groups to indicate the frequency with which they had engaged in policy-influencing strategies over the preceding 12 months. 76.7% participated in public consultations 'very often' or 'fairly often', 68.8% responded to requests for comments and 65% made contact with civil servants. Contacting MSPs or ministers was something done by 43%, while only 27% said that they engaged with Scottish Parliament committees.

Why Lobby Parliament at All?
These findings echo an older observation by Jeremy Richardson and Grant Jordan (1979) that the development of group-government links in policy-making 'robbed' the Westminster parliament of influence; Westminster law-making became a largely formal function – legislative content was bargained in extra parliamentary settings with affected interests. Further, most policy can be made without legislation (i.e. delegated or secondary processes), and where legislation is required the combination of government majorities and a strong party discipline ensures that there is seldom significant amendment. In this context, high levels of group-parliament (London or Edinburgh) contact are best explained by ignorance (groups/corporations do not recognise parliament's irrelevance), the use of parliament as a fallback when objectives have not been met via government consultation, or where elected members' requests for information generate an opportunity for groups to demonstrate their expertise.

An alternative interpretation is that, although most groups recognise the power of government, they 'hedge their bets' and maintain channels of influence in both venues. Indeed, the groups most likely to maintain links with parliament are the 'insider' groups which seek to amend the details of legislation or ensure that decisions reached with government are *not* overturned in parliament. It is the most established and well-resourced groups that maintain a relatively high parliamentary presence. This view is supported to a limited extent by specific examples: public health group pressure in the Scottish Parliament prompted the government to introduce legislation to ban smoking in public places; successful group lobbying of the health committee and opposition parties put further pressure on the government to introduce free personal care for older people; and, the willingness of parliament to say 'no' to legislative measures on adult support and protection in 2007 justified group engagement.

The argument that groups tend to mix influence strategies is also supported, but qualified, by Halpin and MacLeod's study of the policy participants who gave written and/or oral evidence to Scottish parliamentary committees (the data set covers 13,746 acts of evidence given by 3,083 distinct participants to 269 committee bill and inquiry hearings from 1999 to 2007). The first finding (Table 1) is that most participants are not 'interest groups' in the orthodox sense of the term. The dominant type of participant is governmental: sub-units of Scottish central and local government, public sector bodies or agencies. While this is surprising, there is a practical explanation: central government actors have the greatest resources and, in many cases, the greatest *obligation* to inform and respond to committee activity, while local government has more resources to engage than most groups.

Table 1: Distribution of Mobilisation in Connection with Scottish Parliament Committees

	Activity		Participants	
	Frequency	Percent	Frequency	Percent
Government	5,255	38.2	3,738	45.4
Individuals	2,491	18.1	143	1.7
Citizen Groups	2,320	16.9	1,702	20.7
Professional Groups	1,204	8.8	801	9.7
Individual Businesses	779	5.7	627	7.6
Business/Trade Assoc.	760	5.5	505	6.1
Trade Unions	308	2.2	205	2.5
Service Charity	259	1.9	203	2.5
MP, MSP, etc	252	1.8	208	2.5
Religious Org.	107	0.8	82	1.0
Unknown	11	0.1	11	0.1
Total	13,746	100.0	8,225	100.0

There is also a relatively high level of activity by individuals and citizen groups compared to the 'usual suspects' in business and the professions (partly explained by the fact that business groups opposed devolution and took more time to engage). However, this is not necessarily an indicator of sustained wider influence, since giving written evidence is an act of self-selection. If petitions act as a guide, the level of individual activity (143 individuals are responsible for 2,491 responses) suggests serial participation by a small number of driven individuals, while citizen groups appear to be rather narrow and infrequent actors engaged in one or two issues of particular interest. The limited evidence suggests that 'direct' access by disenfranchised groups has been poor. The parliament has been more comfortable with groups acting as proxies.

The 'hedging-bets' argument is perhaps more clearly supported by Table 2, which records the policy participants (but not individuals) with the highest overall levels of activity in committee hearings. Notable here is not only the diversity of interests represented but also the propensity of the major insider groups to engage – including the major government agencies, local authorities, trade unions, professional bodies, business, consumer and environmental groups (complemented by networks of groups such as the 'gang of five' business groups and Environment LINK). Importantly the figures could suggest that parliament *accentuates the bias* towards the 'usual suspects' as much as representing an alternative venue for otherwise excluded groups.

Table 2: Top 28 Policy Participants (1999–2007)

Participant	Activity	Percent	Rank
Scottish Executive (Crown Office, Health Department, Unnamed Dept.)	337	3.0	1
Convention of Scottish Local Authorities (COSLA)	196	1.7	2
Law Society of Scotland	104	0.9	3
Glasgow City Council	87	0.8	4
Edinburgh (City of) Council	78	0.7	5
UNISON Scotland	76	0.7	6
Scottish Trades Union Council/Congress	74	0.7	7
Highlands and Islands Enterprise	74	0.7	8
Association of Chief Police Officers in Scotland	74	0.7	9
Scottish Enterprise	68	0.6	10
Scottish Natural Heritage	67	0.6	11
Highland Council	66	0.6	12
Glasgow University	63	0.6	13
Scottish Consumer Council	61	0.5	14
Federation of Small Businesses	53	0.5	15
Scottish Executive – Minister for Justice	51	0.5	16
Association of Directors of Social Work	47	0.4	17
British Medical Association – Scottish Office, Edinburgh	45	0.4	18
Educational Institute of Scotland (EIS)	44	0.4	19
Edinburgh University	44	0.4	20
Strathclyde University	43	0.4	21
Scottish Environment Protection Agency	43	0.4	22
Dundee City Council	42	0.4	23
Scottish Environment LINK	41	0.4	24
Fife Council	41	0.4	25
Faculty of Advocates, Edinburgh	40	0.4	26
Confederation of British Industry – Scotland	40	0.4	27
South Lanarkshire Council	39	0.3	28
Top 28 Total	2,038	18.1	-
Total	11,255	100.0	-

The Post-2007 Picture

The election of a minority SNP government provided the *potential* for different styles in group-parliament relationships (particularly since the SNP made noises about rejecting governmental reliance on 'establishment' groups). The lack of a governing majority and the scope for cross-party alliances suggests that time spent by groups seeking MSP support may be increasingly valuable. Yet, so far, there is limited evidence of that sort of politics. The new electoral arithmetic (in which no party or coalition controls plenary or committee proceedings) has produced uncertainty but with little evidence of enhanced group influence. The initial rejection of the budget in 2009 was widely seen as ineffective, cumbersome and undesirable politics: this is ironic as such bargaining would be central to 'new politics'. Yet, nothing made majoritarian, imposition politics ('old politics') quite so attractive as a hint of its alternative.

This review suggests that the impact of 'new politics' (at least in the optimistic form presented in the run-up to devolution) is scarcely discernible. But that is not in itself a measure of failure. The question is whether significant groups in Scottish political, social and economic life have ready access to the decision-making forums, not whether the rough pencil sketches of reform were implemented. Political analysis tends to concentrate on weaknesses but the barriers to access are (and were) exaggerated in the pre-devolution portrait of Scottish politics.

Chapter 15

Civil Society and the Parliament

Lindsay Paterson

Two Stories of Modern Scotland

There are two stories about how Scotland gained, or re-gained, its parliament in 1999. One is the rationally democratic, by which an accountable layer was added to an indigenous civil society and an autonomous bureaucracy. This story is about 'devolution'. The other is about a rising of the people against the leaders of civil society. This story is about 'nationalism'. Understanding the parliament's role depends on which story better explains the last 10 years.

The stories largely agree on the pre-1999 history; they differ on interpretation, especially for the 20th century. The 1707 Union worked because it was partial, not incorporating. The governing system was local in its sources of power but still national in its symbolic expressions. The burghs, the presbyterian church, the universities and the sheriff were the chief agents through which the autonomy of local civil society remained intact. Each of these were assembled into concentrated loci of power. The burghs had their national convention. The universities formed a national system responsible for educating the nation's elites. The church had the general assembly, drawing people into debates about the nation's future. Most important was the law, maintained intact by the Union and providing through the senior legal officers the channels of communication between locality and imperial centre in London.

The essence of this structure not only survived into the 20th century but also proved remarkably adaptable to enormous political, social and economic change. Local theocracy gradually became local government in the 19th century as the UK state evolved into one of the most decentralised in Europe. Scottish law and religion continued to provide a national unity of ideas and structures (even when institutionally split as the church came to be). Local government became weaker in the 20th century but there emerged a far more powerful central bureaucracy in the Scottish Office and its quangos, mediating between civil society and the UK state.

Providing leadership were the professions, as in every other European society. Indeed, it was the ordinariness of professional leadership that made it acceptable: if, throughout the UK, professionals were running local government in its increasingly technocratic complexity, and were substituting for politicians in the practical decisions about how this should work nationally, then it caused no difficulty to have that professional governing class organised distinctively in Scotland. It was acceptable provided that these Scottish professionals combined their allegiance to Scottish distinctiveness with loyalty to Britain. This they could do because their creed of universal reason – allocating resources according to the rational principles that constituted the essence of their professionalism – was intimately associated with the ideology of Britishness, admired as the origin of liberalism and a beacon of enlightenment to the world.

The Devolution Story

The different interpretations offered by the two stories relate to the role of professionals. According to the rational-democratic account, they governed well and in accordance with inherited Scottish values. They could establish their authority in the 20th century because they had shown how the state might be used to mitigate poverty, avert disease, modernise industry, civilise the nation through gradually widening education, and stand above the fray of contending passions – especially of sectarian religion – that threatened to bring with mass democracy the mass unreason that was engulfing other parts of Europe. The professionals governed the corporate state of the 1930s onwards with a non-partisan independence. They achieved thereby a great deal, far more than it has become fashionable to credit them with. They did repeatedly modernise the economy. They did alleviate the nation's health through public medicine. They did preside over a smooth transition to a more secular age. And they did build up a system of mass education that, by the 1980s, was providing to a majority of children in secondary schools some access to the fruits of liberal culture that only a tiny minority of their forebears could have acquired from the old universities.

They also defended most of this from the Conservative governments of the 1980s and 1990s. This was crucial for their own conversion to self-government, and brings us to the essence of this first story about how the parliament came about. The old system, it is claimed, was working well until the 1960s. Indeed, its not being evidently broken might explain the lack of enthusiasm for the Assembly that was offered in 1979. The networks of committees and agencies, staffed by disinterested professionals, and drawing upon the distilled wisdom of civil society, were still able to represent the nation to the state. But all that then changed, not because Thatcher was antagonistic to Scotland but because she distrusted any structures that promoted professional self-interest. In reducing these influences, she also inadvertently reduced Scotland's, and accidentally thus pushed the Scottish professionals into concluding that the governing system had to be modernised again. This time, though, there was a wider sense that society had to be democratised. Scotland (like everywhere else in Europe), because better educated, had become less deferential and more interested in individual rights. So the modernising could not avoid being through an elected legislature, but its continuity with the old would be through it being grounded in civil society.

In this first story, in other words, the parliament returns Scotland to the 1950s, as it were, modified only by the need to do this in a more democratic way. Encouraging people to ask questions of governing groups was not the same as asking them to supplant the old networks, and the professionals leading the Constitutional Convention from the late-1980s never doubted that consultation would re-entrench them in their historical role of national leadership.

The Nationalism Story
The other story disagrees most sharply. The reform led by welfare-state professionals is seen as unwarranted caution. Allegiance to both Scotland and Britain is hypocrisy and dependence. Professional self-confidence is, echoing Thatcher, self-interest. The purpose of a parliament was precisely to remove these leaders of civil society from the influence that they had not earned, that they had exercised with unpardonable condescension, and that they had squandered because of their alleged unwillingness to challenge the norms or policies not only of the Thatcher government but also of all that preceded it.

The greatest exponent of this story is Tom Nairn, but there are also three strands to it beyond his writings. The most obvious is on the anarchic left, and may be dated in its modern version from the writings of Hugh MacDiarmid in the 1920s and 1930s. He excoriated the Scottish bourgeoisie, earning himself the complaint which James Mitchell quotes from the leader of moderate nationalism in the middle of the century, John MacCormick: 'politically one of the greatest handicaps with which any national movement could have been burdened'. A second strand evolved from that one, as a cultural critique of Scottish elites that drew upon the anti-colonial rhetoric of the 1960s. Probably the most influential writers in this vein have been Craig Beveridge and Ronald Turnbull, but the sentiment came to permeate the leftist cultural activism that provided the real energy to Scottish debates in the 1980s. The third strand is quite different from these, and is exemplified by the Tory historian and undeviating supporter of home rule, Michael Fry, who derided the Scottish welfare-state establishment for its smug corporatism. Each of these strands has always been outside the respectable nationalism of the SNP: at least since the 1960s, the party has never been the main carrier of the most searching nationalist critiques of Scottish society and government.

The Victory of Devolution
What, then – as between these two accounts – has happened since 1999? Almost without caveat, the answer is a clear victory for the first. The parliament has become a forum for civil society, especially for its articulate professional segments. According to research by Darren Halpin and Graeme Baxter, there has been little change since before 1999 in the kind of organisations that have taken part in public consultations. These have been dominated by established lobbying groups, representative groups of specialist interests (including commercial business), and organisations of professionals such as doctors,

teachers, housing experts and planners. The number of individuals taking part in consultations did grow, but they were concentrated in a small proportion of the consultations, and their submissions often took the form of standard letters sponsored by lobbying organisations. According to the research, the largest category taking part in governmental consultations (over four out of 10 groups which contributed) were other organisations in the public sector. It would be a rash politician who sought to challenge the authority of these professional networks.

Prior to these public consultations have been the specialist working parties through which the Scottish civil service has overcome its lack of policy-making expertise. Consultation documents have been produced by committees dominated by professionals; then the public responses to the consultations have come from the professional bodies in which these same people are prominent. Academics have been particularly important in this respect. They have shaped debate through books such as the present one; even when they have questioned professional influence, they have done so from the same sources of rational and bureaucratic authority as explain that very status.

Members of the Scottish Parliament would be unlikely to demur, because most of them come from that same professional world. In the 1999-2003 session, two-thirds had been educated in Scottish universities and colleges. According to research by Mark Shephard and colleagues, only 2% had had any experience in a working class job and only 12% had been a trade union official; the remainder had had working experience only in the professions.[1] The MSPs and professionals thus shared an assumptive world. They shared this, too, with the senior civil servants, two-thirds of whom were educated in this same way, and who absorbed advisers from the policy networks and the universities.

Professionals are much more impressed by the parliament's record than people who are more marginal to power, and so have become its public bulwark. We may illustrate this using the 2007 Scottish Social Attitudes Survey by comparing the views of two groups at opposite ends of the scale of influence: people working in high professional or managerial occupations and who have a higher-education qualification (8% of the population), and people in semi-routine or routine occupations with education below the level of lower secondary (14%). 67% of these professionals thought the parliament was giving people a greater say in government in contrast to 34% of the other group. The proportions believing that Scotland's voice in the UK was being strengthened were 66% and 48%. The level of discontent with the parliament's current powers was the reverse of these: 54% of professionals wanted more powers but 77% of the other group. The two groups differed markedly on many other social views, indicating how sanguine about society in general the professionals were: 70% against 27%

[1] M. Shephard, N. McGarvey & M. Cavanagh (2001), 'New Scottish Parliament, New Scottish Parliamentarians?', Journal of Legislative Studies, 2, pp. 79-104.

believed that most people may be trusted; 38% against 76% believed that 'there is one law for the rich and one for the poor'; 47% against 71% favoured censorship to uphold moral values; 79% against 58% voted in the 2007 elections.

The almost utopian rhetoric which pervaded the campaigning for a parliament – inspired especially by the second of our two stories – might then lead us to ask whether this alienation of marginalised social groups from it might in the long term threaten its legitimacy. That may be so, but probably not. A pragmatic reason to doubt it is that these same surveys show that the marginal group is even more alienated from the UK state, the only viable alternative to home rule. A deeper reason is summed up by a comment from Bernard Levin on utopianism in general: 'utopians are inured to disappointment; … there are always fellow-utopians to throw a life-belt to those struggling in the water of broken promises'. That is presumably why the typical response of the marginalised to their disappointment is to support greater powers for the parliament, not its abolition. In any case, the general support which people give to the very existence of the parliament, despite all this, is probably evidence that they subscribe vaguely to Thomas Carlyle's view of democracy, which was that the most important right is not to participate but to be ruled well. Here that means being ruled by the very experts who are now most sympathetic to the current parliament's format.

This outcome was perhaps unsurprising during the parliament's first eight years, when the executive was dominated by the Labour Party, which had been the main exponent of the first story and the natural political home of professionals in general. But the SNP in government after 2007 has not tried to disrupt any of this. Constrained by being in a minority, they enthusiastically followed the consensual ethos of doing little to challenge the authority of the dominant professional interests. A politically symbolic moment for this tendency was during the financial crisis of autumn 2008, when there would have been scope to have used the collapse of two of Scotland's most apparently venerable institutions to question the complacency of the Edinburgh professional establishment. The SNP chose not to do so, praising the disintegrating banks and blaming the disaster on speculators outside Scotland, or on the UK state (later extending the blame to a few prominent bankers but not to whole Scottish institutions). More generally, the striking feature of the SNP approach since 1999 has been its desire to appear respectable. Conscious that they lack Labour's dense networks of supporters in the professional classes, they have shown no inclination to adopt the Nairn line according to which the problem was the professional classes' craven unionism. The approach taken by John MacCormick has won, and the MacDiarmid–Nairn critique has drifted even further away from the party mainstream than it ever was. The sceptic might conclude that what Nairn called 'backyard autonomy' – as well as a new kind of corporatism – seems safe in their hands.

Conclusion: The Enduring Power of Scotland's Civil Society

So self-government has not challenged the power of civil society or the authority of professionals. More of these people may have appeared in public, for example giving evidence to parliamentary committees. Some may be shifting their partisan allegiance away from Labour, working on social policy with the SNP government even if not sharing its views on independence. A few more unestablished interests may be intervening in consultations, although not many. But generally what we have had is a vindication of the power of ancient networks. This may or may not be a good thing: the heirs to the two stories of origins take forward their interpretation into current judgements. What we have not had is a revolution, whether of social structure (which was never likely), or of the power of organised interests, or of the authority of the professional technocracy – including academics – in public debate. The Scottish Parliament, faithful to the rational democratic story of how it came about, has indeed given us no more (but also no less) than the 1950s Scottish governing system made more democratically transparent.

Chapter 16

The Media and Parliament

Brian McNair

For decades, indeed centuries, the Scottish media have been a source of national pride. Alongside the education system, the Church of Scotland and the legal apparatus, the media have been rightly viewed as a distinctive Scottish cultural institution, a key part of what makes Scotland a nation rather than a region. Scotland has long sustained, per capita, one of the richest and most diverse media systems in the world, encapsulating a heady mix of local newspapers such as the *West Highland Free Press*, national [i.e., Scotland-wide] newspapers and broadcast outlets such as BBC Scotland and *The Scotsman*, and UK-based media with Scottish editions such as *The Sun* and the *Daily Mail*. These media have reflected and fuelled what is in turn a distinctive Scottish political identity separate from, though connected with, that of the United Kingdom as a whole. There has, for example, been no major paper with a pro-Tory editorial line north of the border for longer than most of us can remember, reflecting (and perhaps contributing to) the Conservative Party's poor showing in successive Scottish elections.

The Scottish Media: A Watchdog without Teeth
The roots of this distinctive media environment lie in Scotland's history as a nation conscious and protective of its own culture. Arthur Herman's book on the Scottish Enlightenment shows how important Scottish intellectual life – and by extension the media which allowed it to flourish – were to the development of democratic and liberal thought not only in Britain and Europe, but the United States of America and beyond. The coffee house culture of free thinking and discussion identified by Jurgen Habermas as a crucible of bourgeois democracy was prominent in late 18th century and early 19th century Edinburgh, and articulated in periodicals such as the *Edinburgh Review*. Scotland gave birth to some of the oldest newspapers still publishing anywhere in the world, such as the *Aberdeen Press and Journal* (1748) and *The Herald* (launched in 1783 as the *Glasgow Advertiser*).

Until devolution, however, and with growing urgency in the 18 years of UK Tory government preceding it, there was a sense of something amiss in the national story covered by the Scottish media. Scotland was a nation, yes, but not a nation state. Its government was in the hands of the Westminster parliament, its political direction at the mercy of whichever party ruled there. Margaret Thatcher's introduction of the poll tax in Scotland, one year before it became law in England, became a symbol of the vulnerability of Scottish society and politics to the whims of an ideologically hostile Westminster majority. The Scottish media, unlike their London-based counterparts, lacked a national constituent assembly within which these and other UK government-imposed measures could be scrutinised and challenged. As professionals eager to perform their fourth estate role, Scottish political journalists were emasculated by the fact that they had no parliament to report, just the Scottish Office, a department of the Westminster government.

Then came New Labour and devolution. A Scottish Parliament was established in 1999, and a new era for the Scottish media began. The parliament established by the 1998 Scotland Act was not a government with all of the powers accruing to nation states, but it was a major constitutional advance on the Scottish Office. Among its most enthusiastic supporters were Scottish journalists, in the belief that now at last they had a representative government of sufficient power and authority to really get their teeth into. If the journalist in a democracy is ideally cast as a watchdog, now they had something to watch over. Overnight, it seemed, Scottish politics had become bigger, more relevant, a story worthy of the best journalistic talents. Scottish politics would be galvanised, and so would the Scottish media. Democracy would be strengthened.

In response to devolution the Scottish media beefed up their editorial resource devoted to politics. A Scottish parliamentary lobby formed, and there was substantial investment in providing reporting facilities, by media organisations and politicians alike. An entirely new zone of the Scottish public sphere came into being, staffed by the best and the brightest of Scottish journalists, focused on this new parliament on which the eyes of Scotland, the UK and the world were trained.

Ten years on, though, and all is not well. The Scottish media, both print and broadcast, are in a state of crisis. A large part of that crisis is caused by the global structural shift from print and analogue broadcasting – the great carrier media of the 20th century – to the internet and digital TV. Newspaper circulations in Scotland are in decline, as they are in every advanced capitalist country, as readers abandon print and move online to mobile platforms such as PCs, telephones and PDAs. In the UK as a whole that decline has been around 3% year on year for a decade. But in Scotland it has been higher – 6% for many titles in 2008. This can be explained in part by the very richness and diversity of the Scottish media marketplace, where UK-based papers with well-resourced Scottish editions such as *The Sun* take market share from indigenous titles such as *The Record*. *The Sunday Herald* competes not only with *Scotland On Sunday*, but all the London-based Sundays too, several of which take their Scottish readers very seriously indeed.

As for broadcasting, Scottish media organisations suffer from the same technological and cultural shifts as their UK parents and partners. BBC Scotland struggles to remake itself for the digital century, and will succeed, but STV faces major and as yet unresolved revenue problems in the wake of analogue switch-off. Throughout the sector there is gloom and pessimism, and despite the good work of the Scottish Broadcasting Commission in identifying issues and challenges, the future of Scottish broadcasting remains, as of this writing, unclear.

On the other hand, Scottish media have for the first time had a proper democratic parliament to report on, a parliament now infused with the drama of a nationalist government committed to independence, if not now, then when the fear induced by the credit crunch and the global recession has become a memory and we get back to politics as usual. One might expect the media in Scotland to benefit from this reconfigured political landscape, to have gained audiences rather than shed them as they have. But the parliament too has its problems. Principally, that of poor public participation and esteem. In the first Scottish parliamentary elections of 1999, just over 58% of the people voted. In 2003 the figure was down to 49.4%, and in 2007 up a little to 51.72%. After the first flush of popular enthusiasm, it seems, the Scottish people have lost a degree of interest in their parliament and its MSPs.

Levels of democratic participation are affected by many factors, and causality is impossible to prove. But there is widespread consensus amongst political scientists, media scholars, journalists and politicians alike that the performance of the political media may have had something to do with the marked decline in voting rates seen in the UK and elsewhere in the western world in the last decade (notwithstanding that these have come up again in the most recent UK and US elections). Critics of the media have talked of the 'corrosive cynicism' of political journalists, the 'hyperadversarialism' of the Paxman-esque interviewers, the relentless focus on the negative which has characterised political news in recent times. And in Scotland there has certainly been plenty of that in coverage of the parliament since 1999.

Reporting the Parliament, 1999-2009

The trouble started even before the parliament was constructed, with the controversy surrounding the appointment of Enric Miralles and the subsequent huge increases in the budget for the building. While the Miralles controversy was mainly aesthetic (and to some extent procedural) and quickly faded when people saw the beauty of the building, the cost issue dominated the news agenda in the first years of the parliament's life and, as with the Millennium Dome in London, cast a shadow over the 'project'. Scottish politicians only had themselves to blame for this, given Donald Dewar's reckless assertion before the work began that a new parliament could be had for less than £50 million. The final bill of more than £400 million represented a 900% over-run on that early back-of-a-napkin estimate, and was widely and justifiably reported in the Scottish media as a product of mismanagement.

Earlier in the parliament's life, while it still sat in its temporary home on the Mound, the first of a series of alleged corruption stories affecting MSPs emerged. In August 1999 *The Observer* made allegations that Beattie Media, a public relations and lobbying company employing amongst others the son of senior New Labour minister John Reid was using its familial and other Labour contacts to attract parliamentary lobbying business. The firm could deliver special access to key decision-makers in the parliament, it claimed (according to *The Observer*), and thus advantage in the competition for public sector contracts and spending.

The story became a Scottish and UK-wide media scandal, and while John Reid successfully deflected accusations of nepotism and worse, it tarnished the parliament, virtually from the outset, with the image of shady dealings, old pals' networks, and Labour mafias at the heart of the devolution project. Scottish politics as usual, in other words, rather than the promised new dawn of accessible, accountable government.

Further, even juicier scandals followed. Donald Dewar's successor as First Minister, Henry McLeish, was forced to resign in 2001 following allegations that he had improperly sublet his constituency office. Not to be outdone, the Conservative leader in the parliament, David McLetchie, quit after being caught spending £11,500 of taxpayers' money on taxi fares while on party business. More recently, Labour leader Wendy Alexander was forced to resign after admitting a breach of electoral funding regulations, this in the context of a concurrent UK-wide scandal about Labour's campaign which ended Gordon Brown's brief honeymoon period as Prime Minister.

The scandal of the parliament building returned in the form of a 2006 documentary about the project commissioned by the BBC, at a reported cost of £3 million, from the Wark Clements media company. Controversy surrounded the fact that Kirsty Wark, a close friend of Donald Dewar, as well as a senior BBC news journalist and thus with an obligation to impartiality in all things political, had been appointed by Dewar to the committee which appointed Enric Miralles as the project architect. She was also, it then emerged in the increasingly gleeful Scottish media, a close friend of Jack McConnell, by then First Minister. Photographs of her and McConnell sharing holidays in Mallorca appeared in the Scottish papers, and Wark's position at the BBC was called into question (as well as the potential for conflict of interest around her involvement with *The Gathering Place* documentary). Again, Scottish media audiences were presented with the appearance of a clique of insiders extending from the parliament to other sectors of society, and using their connections for personal and political advantage.

Most scandalous of all, however, was the Tommy Sheridan saga, which included the full gamut of sex, lies and videotape, and as of this writing remains the subject of legal action. The details of the scandal affecting the leader of the Scottish Socialist party, who also happened to be one of Scotland's most outspoken MSPs, are less important than the fact that for months, indeed years, it flooded the Scottish media with tales of sexual degeneracy, comradely back-stabbing, macho left posturing and alleged perjury.

These examples do not exhaust the flow of scandal generated by the Scottish parliament in its first decade, but they may help to explain the less than whole-hearted enthusiasm with which the Scottish electorate now treats the institution it so widely welcomed just a decade ago. Media coverage of the parliament has represented its members as financially and morally corrupt, and suggested that they form part of the same old cliques which, critics assert, have dominated Scottish politics for decades. These may be unfair and inaccurate perceptions of the quality of the majority of MSPs, but even the most forgiving of observers may be forgiven for thinking there is at least a grain of truth in them.

There is no point in criticising the Scottish media for this coverage, even if it might be very damaging to the parliament's public standing. News organisations in Scotland, as elsewhere, are competitive animals, driven by news values which stress the dramatic, the negative, the conflictual. Corruption when exposed is bound to become the subject of scandal, which is why politicians in the modern world of always-on, hyper-active media are well advised to ensure that they are free of it, and secure against the accusation of it. The citizen, indeed, is entitled to expect his or her media to report these issues fully, if fairly.

Missing the Wood for the Trees

And with all this scandal to report, who can blame the Scottish media for under-reporting the good news about the parliament? The Labour-Liberal government which lost power to the SNP in 2007 with the narrowest of margins had presided over a period of respectable, if not world-beating economic growth. Scotland's perennial problems of welfare state dependency, alcohol-fuelled violence and social deprivation had not been cured, nor noticeably improved, but neither was the story of the first decade of devolved government one of disastrous incompetence. The rise of the SNP between 2003 and 2007 had much to do with the war in Iraq and other UK political factors over which the Scottish government had little control, but it is reasonable to speculate that the constant flow of scandal and corruption stories about the parliament flowing from the Scottish media from 1999 onwards had at least something to do with the perception that it was 'time for a change'.

Chapter 17

Centre and Locality in Scottish Politics: From Bi- to Tri-partite Relations

Neil McGarvey

When local government is discussed two contrasting narratives are often presented. The first projects a story of centralisation and declining local autonomy, the second one of partnership, interdependency and a respect for boundaries between centre and locality. The post-devolution story of Scottish local government is a nuanced one which does not fit neatly into either narrative.

The old pre-devolution bi-partite structure between the Convention of Scottish Local Authorities (COSLA) and the Scottish Office has been replaced with new tri-partite relations involving local government interests, the Scottish Government and the Scottish Parliament. But in a key respect there is a continuity: local councils have the same constitutional, statutory and legal limitations on the extent of their independent activities as before devolution. They are constitutionally just as subordinate to Scotland's devolved institutions as they were to the Scottish Office and the UK parliament. Focusing just on constitutional structure however ignores the changed political dynamic of relations between centre and locality. The elections of the Scottish Parliament and the accountability of the Scottish government to it introduce a vastly different context for local government.

The addition of democratic politics to the Scottish 'centre' has extended ministerial and parliamentary oversight, and created a new generation of 129 politicians in the Scottish Parliament who, as a matter of course, concern themselves with the issues which Scottish local councils retain responsibility for. Pre-devolution, the Scottish Office had only five ministers. The volume of legislation impacting on local councils and the scale and proximity of parliamentary scrutiny has increased dramatically. The Scottish Parliament has created a more open, inclusive, pluralistic and accessible governmental environment. COSLA has moved from a position of opposition to one of constructive dialogue. The rhetoric of partnership has been consistent in the first 10 years.

Before Devolution

Before outlining the new tri-partite relations of central-local government, it is necessary to reflect on the pre-devolution structure. Between 1979 and 1997 the Conservative-run Scottish Office operated, at times, in a rather unilateral fashion, imposing its own policy agenda on local government. Policies such as the right-to-buy, rate capping, compulsory competitive tendering, the poll tax, and local government reorganisation in 1995-96 were imposed despite strong opposition. Thus by the late 1990s, as Charlie Gordon put it:

> The defensive struggles against the Tory social and economic policies, fought by Scottish local government from 1979 to 1997, had strengthened the attraction of a constitutional solution which had been waiting in the political wings all those years.

COSLA, like other political institutions in Scotland, viewed the parliament as a potential safeguard and shield against any future right of centre Conservative UK government. It played a key role in the Scottish Constitutional Convention, providing both operational and political support to the campaign for home rule. By the devolution referendum in 1997, despite some concerns that devolution could easily lead to centralisation, COSLA was very supportive of the creation of the new parliament. Scottish local government was part of what Ian Lang described as the 'congealing consensus' in Scottish civic society in favour of home rule.

The Tri-partite Relationship of Local Government, Scottish Parliament and Scottish Government

However, the concern that the new parliament would over-shadow localities has not proved to be totally unfounded. Between 1979 and 1997, COSLA and Scottish local authorities could legitimately claim to be the *only* authentic democratic voice based in Scotland. That is no longer the case. One need only reflect on the coverage of the parliamentary and local elections to be aware of the comparative esteem of each in media circles.

However, what the parliament has created is a new arena of central-local politics. Scottish central-local relations have moved from a bi-partite to a tri-partite structure. The 1998 Scotland Act devolved all responsibility for the functions of powers of local government to the Scottish Parliament. In the white paper which followed the 'Yes, Yes' vote in the referendum, assurances were made by the UK government pre-devolution that it did not expect the Scottish Parliament to accumulate and take powers and functions from localities. To alleviate any fears of centralisation in local government circles, the Labour-run Scottish Office (1997–99) appointed Neil McIntosh to chair a commission examining the Scottish Parliament's potential impact on local government.

In 2001 the newly created Scottish executive and COSLA agreed a partnership framework. It contained a commitment, on the part of the executive, to consult COSLA and, where appropriate, individual councils, on 'all proposals which affect or might affect the structure, role and functions and financing of local government'. However, the partnership framework did not prevent some high-profile occasions when ministers failed to consult local government e.g. on electoral reform, the proposals to establish a Scottish strategic transport authority or a single correctional agency and on the extension of ministerial powers to deal with failing schools. The 'partnership' looked very one-sided.

> **Box 1: Key Features of the Scottish Executive–COSLA Partnership Framework 2001**
> - Principle of respect – parity of esteem and principle of subsidiarity
> - Recognition of distinct and complementary roles of executive (developing public policy at national level and bringing forward legislation) and councils (ascertaining need of communities, prioritising, planning, co-ordinating and delivering local services within statutory framework)
> - Commitment to partnership working on strategic issues
> - Active involvement of local government at the formative stage on principle and practice of any proposals that impact on local government
> - Executive to facilitate (minimum 12-week) consultation on proposals affecting local government, including financial impacts
> - Proposals which impact on local government will include detailed description and estimated impact of any financial burdens
> - Regular meetings between ministers and COSLA

The McIntosh Report had other wider repercussions, most notably the Kerley Report which followed. This resulted in the introduction of the single transferable vote (STV) electoral system for local elections in 2007, resulting in a more pluralistic party environment in Scottish local authorities. At the last count, there were 17 different configurations of minority/coalition administration arrangements in Scotland's 32 council chambers. That said, the narrow base from which Scotland's political class is recruited has shown no sign of broadening – the dominant councillor caricature being that 'he' is usually white, middle class and middle aged rings as true in 2009 as it did in 1999.

Council democratic and managerial practices have also been changing. Various initiatives have opened up councils to other institutions operating locally. Community planning is a policy which was piloted pre-devolution, however since 1999 it has evolved and was given statutory basis in 2003. It involves local councils coming together with other public sector agencies in their local area at a strategic level to develop shared objectives. The 2003 Act also gives councils a new power to promote or improve well-being. However, this was not quite the power of general competence COSLA had long campaigned for. The 2003 Act also allowed ministers to use preliminary notices and enforcement powers to police this new duty of well-being. It should be noted that the centre has, to date, resisted the temptation to go down the English route of intervention in 'failing' services.

Indeed, the contrast with England has become more stark. The Blairite (like the Thatcherite) thrust of reform did not have quite the same impact in Scotland as it did south of the border, though the same overarching narratives of reinvention, re-engineering, renewal and modernisation have been apparent in Scotland. However, changed party political dynamics (in particular the lack of a credible right-of-centre alternative), a distinct civil society rooted in a public sector ethos and Scotland's distinct 'national world of local government' have ensured local government has not followed the UK agenda. For example, the English agenda of elected mayors simply did not register in Scotland. Policy labels (e.g. best value) may be identical but the actual processes surrounding them are very different in character in Scotland. The existence of the Scottish Parliament has accentuated pre-existing policy process and output differences with England.

That said, the Scottish Parliament, to date, has shown no willingness to engage in a radical re-working of the conventional paradigm of UK central-local relations. The constitutional position remains one of subordination. The Scottish Parliament can legislate to re-draw boundaries, remove functions or even abolish local authorities. Increasing central regulation, scrutiny and a degree of mistrust between local government and the civil service was a theme of early post-devolution research 1999-2007. Overall, the constitutional contours of the central-local relationship remain similar north and south of the border.

However, the new tri-partite political relationship between locality and centre is more nuanced, complex and interdependent than a simple outline of its legal contours. The cohesiveness of both locality and the centre of Scottish politics is exaggerated by the phrase 'central-local' relations. The environment of policymaking in Scotland is not as self-contained as a simple reading of the 1998 Scotland Act would suggest – the UK Treasury, for example, was a key player in the large scale voluntary transfer of Glasgow city council's housing stock.

The governmental part of the centre, despite post-1999 efforts to build up its corporate central policy-making capability, remains a collection of separate departments and associated policy networks. Scottish education, for example, has long been a rather autonomous policy network. Also a distinction has to be made between Scottish government ministers and its permanent bureaucracy. There remains a lingering degree of reciprocal suspicion and distrust between local government and the civil service.

The elected part of the Scottish centre, parliament and its parties and committees, represent new arenas and networks for central-local interaction. The 'local' is usually read as COSLA, but it is in reality an umbrella group seeking to represent the pluralistic political interests of 32 directly-elected local authorities of varying political complexions. It, like the Scottish government, has both a permanent bureaucratic and political side. Moreover, there are other notable institutions representing local interests competing for influence – the Scottish branch of the Society of Local Authority Chief Executives (SOLACE), the Improvement Service as well as national professional associations in policy areas (e.g. Educational Institute for Scotland) and trade unions (e.g. UNISON).

Despite its post-devolution additional complexity the national world of local government in Scotland remains a much smaller, cohesive arena than at UK level. Since 1999, a combination of several factors such as party links between governmental, parliamentary and local politicians, a significant degree of social policy consensus and shared local government experience linking local government, parliament and Scottish government, have combined to produce a national policy-making environment where there is a degree of shared ownership of policy. The Scottish government, parliament and COSLA have emphasised sharing priorities as regards issues such as social inclusion, health improvement and educational outcomes.

Relationships since 2007

Since the 2007 election, community planning partnerships have been utilised to allow councils and other agencies to develop single outcome agreements (SOAs). SOAs are the latest in a long list of policy initiatives aimed at improving the rationality, efficiency, co-ordination, outputs and outcomes of public service delivery in Scotland. Although SOAs are the flagship policy emerging from the concordat agreed between COSLA and the Scottish government in 2007, the concept has been lingering on the agenda of central-local relations since a Scottish executive/COSLA task force report in 2000. Implicit within them is the notion that some of the 15 national outcomes outlined by the Scottish government will be reflected in local authority desired public policy outcomes i.e. there is a clear link between national and local priorities and a sense of common ground between both.

The 2007 concordat agreement was designed to symbolically signal a shift from the 1999-2007 era of incremental and creeping centralisation with new legislation, directives, ring-fenced budgets, regulatory regimes and other such devices reducing the autonomy of local authorities. It emphasises a 'new relationship' and 'mutual respect and partnership' as well as 'a fundamental shift in the relationship between the Scottish government and local government'. The Scottish government were emphasising the movement towards a less prescriptive and interventionist approach. However, you do get a sense of *déjà vu* when you read it – some of the language is very familiar to a previous one signed in 2001.

That said, local government has appeared closer and more in tune with central government since 2007. Reduced ring-fencing, council tax freezes, the first two rounds of SOAs signalled a more genuine partnership. The concordat represents both a symbolic and real shift in tri-partite relations. The Scottish government, recognising the parliamentary arithmetic would not equate to the smooth passage of legislative reform, has opted to work with local government. This has marginalised parliament in the tri-partite structure. The abolition of much of the ring-fencing of local authority funding, marked a break from the 1999-2007 period of creeping regulation, encroachment and oversight. The

Box 2: Key Features of the Scottish Government–COSLA Concordat 2007

- A commitment that the Scottish government will not undertake structural reform of local government during the term of this parliament
- That there will be a move to a SOA for every council, based on the agreed set of national outcomes (underpinned by agreed national indicators)
- SOA processes will be supported by streamlined external scrutiny and effective performance management systems, and more focused and proportionate inspection regimes replacing the myriad of existing systems
- The Scottish government will reduce substantially the number of separate funding streams to local government
- That local authorities agree to deliver on a specified set of commitments from within the funding provided
- Local authorities will be able to retain – for the first time – all their efficiency savings to re-deploy against ongoing pressures
- That COSLA and the Scottish government will put in place arrangements jointly to oversee and monitor the new partnership and, as part of this, to assess how the new arrangements are working and how each side is fulfilling the commitments made

post devolution trend of the hypothecation of funding for specified areas has been reversed. The SNP minority government, at a strategic level, has prioritised establishing a close relationship with COSLA and local government – recognising that political objectives could be more readily achieved through this route than by seeking coalitions to legislate through the parliament. SOAs engender notions of 'joint accountability' between centre and locality.

Concerns about local democracy and autonomy remain post-devolution, although they have been alleviated by the genuine proximity and consultation which takes place at national level in both government and parliament. Indeed in terms of the dynamics of power on the 'local' side one could argue that the 'centre' (in the form of COSLA and other organisations like the Scottish branch of Local Authority Chief Executives (SOLACE) and the newly created Improvement Service) of it have gained power at the expense of the 32 local authorities. SOAs have been driven by a combination of national *political* leadership and COSLA. The 'national' representatives of local authorities are heavily involved in policy processes. Implicit in SOAs is local acceptance of Scottish government national policy outcomes. The leadership of COSLA have been willing to forego some aspects of local autonomy in return for an enhanced national policy advisory and developmental role.

In summary, the post-devolution experience of local government in Scotland does not fit neatly into a 'partnership' or 'centralisation' narrative. Where centralisation has occurred it has been within local government and often with the compliance of COSLA. Post-2007, the Scottish government, recognising the potential difficulty it has in achieving its policy objectives via the legislative route – due to its minority status – has reached out to local government. It has reconfigured the government-parliament-local government tri-partite structure as it has sought to work beyond parliament. The result has been that the access and influence of 'national' local government interests have been accentuated.

Chapter 18

Quangos, Agencies and the Scottish Parliament

Richard Parry

The role of the Scottish Parliament was to assert local, continuous control over the government of devolved services. The 400-mile gap in accountability that became so contentious in the 1980s and 1990s was to be closed by local ministers in constant attendance on the parliament, with a vast increase in legislative and investigatory capacity. The modalities of the parliament's work were developed afresh by the Consultative Steering Group and were not inhibited by Westminster precedents. In many respects this potential has been used well and the accountability function of the legislative branch enforced conscientiously.

There is also another form of distancing – not geographical but organisational, by placing the structures of government at arm's length from ministers and parliament. This was an important theme of UK government in the 1970s and 1980s, partly designed to manipulate downwards the number of civil service 'bureaucrats' or 'pen-pushers' and partly a search for better corporate governance, in which managerially-skilled chief executives were answerable to a board of directors with the right expertise to scrutinise and plan. The Consultative Steering Group did not anticipate any problems that these structures might cause the parliament; the chapter on accountability in the report discussed 'whether questions should be acceptable only if they relate to matters for which the executive is responsible', but this was in the context of reserved powers. The report noted that a public forum they had held in Galashiels had raised the issue that quangos and appointments to them should be made more accountable but did not discuss the point further.

Quangos in Scotland
This was a typical non-reaction at the time. In the executive as opposed to the legislative branch, the devolved Scottish government was a concept-taker rather than a concept-maker. The wider universe of the public sector in devolved areas inherited, and has continued to use, the same modalities as the UK government. To be specific, the Scottish Parliament has continued to scrutinise the following kinds of organisations where there might be some compromise of their rights to question and investigate because they are not ministerial departments:

1. Civil service agencies, notably the Scottish Prison Service, the Scottish Courts Administration, Historic Scotland and the Scottish Student Awards Agency. These will typically have management boards and

sometimes non-executive directors and are somewhat detached from ministerial control, although their staff are civil servants and Westminster-derived protocols make it difficult for ministers to use their chief executives to shield themselves from questioning about them

2. Health service bodies (trusts were abolished in 2004, but territorial and special health boards continue under strong ministerial direction)

3. Non-departmental public bodies (NDPB) of an executive and/or advisory nature (including 'non-ministerial departments' like the Office of the Scottish Charities Regulator); some of these have been given the status of company limited by guarantee and some will require legislation to alter – the clue to their status is the appointment of the board of directors by Scottish ministers

4. Public corporations – Scottish Water, Caledonian MacBrayne, Highlands and Islands airports (operationally independent in day-to-day management); and, at greatest distance from ministerial control

5. Local public spending bodies (recipients of central government funds like universities and housing associations that lie outside the legally-defined public sector and so are immune from direct questioning)

These bodies dwarf the 6,000 staff in the core of the Scottish government; in 2008 about 160,000 worked in the health service, 40,000 in public corporations and NDPBs and 10,000 in civil service agencies.

'Quango culls' have been tried by both Scottish administrations. In 2001, the Labour-Liberal Democrat executive proposed to shed 43 out of 113 bodies studied. Their report had an analytical structure in which accountability issues figured prominently: they stated that 'where there is a very strong argument for ministers remaining *directly* accountable to parliament for the *execution* of a function ... interposing an unnecessary barrier between ministers and those carrying out the function conflicts with the principle of direct accountability'. They also offered to inform committee conveners when they appointed a new high-level task force. They greatly reduced the number of health bodies and appointments by abolishing health service trusts, a bold move not done elsewhere in the UK. The SNP launched its own cull under the banner of *Simplifying Public Services*; on 30 January 2008, Alex Salmond announced a reduction of 52 in the 199 national organisations. The arguments presented for this were on the desirability of a 'leaner, more strategic' landscape able to promote value for money and user focus. Accountability issues were much less prominent and were presented in the context of 'effective sponsorship arrangements', a euphemism for government control.

Parliamentary Scrutiny of the Scottish Quangos

How has the parliament responded to this? In one sense, there is no great problem: where public money is involved the parliament will seek to scrutinise whatever body spends it, using its legal powers to require any person to give evidence or produce documents 'concerning any subject for which any member of the Scottish executive has general responsibility'. This parallels the inclination of the public auditors to go after the destination and use of public money even when it is channelled into non-ministerial or non-public bodies. The Audit committee (now Public Audit) has reported frequently on health boards, further education colleges and Scottish Enterprise on this basis.

One potential problem of quango status – the inability to get answers to parliamentary questions about operational matters – has not been significant as ministers have sought to satisfy members by reporting information and action on the issue raised. For agencies the formula used by ministers in parliamentary answers is 'I have asked [chief executive] to respond. His/her response is....'. For the health service, answers about local issues tend to be direct and complete, though sometimes state that 'the data requested are not held centrally' or have 'been supplied by NHS National Services Scotland'. For public corporations a typical response is 'this is an operational matter for Scottish Enterprise. I will ask its chief executive to write to you in this regard'; the answer is not reported to parliament but the weight of the government is put behind satisfying the member.

In terms of Scottish Parliament activity, one inhibition is that there is no equivalent of the House of Commons public administration committee, which only came into being in 1997 and whose area of work was not addressed by the Consultative Steering Group. Subject committees tend to be more interested in the substance of policy than in organisational change. The non-subject committees have not used the possibility in their remits to look at structures – equal opportunities has not explored such issues, and standards, procedures and public appointments has concentrated on allegations against MSPs and has not used its responsibility for the commissioner for public appointments to issue general reports on the universe of quangos that she regulates. In the former procedures committee's important review of the *Founding Principles of the Scottish Parliament* in 2003 the closest it came to any engagement with the issue is an assertion that 'in addition to holding ministers to account, parliament scrutinises the civil service and non-departmental public bodies (NDPBs) in the performance of their duties.' The audit committee's report of 2003 *How Government Works in Scotland* asked the executive to examine whether corporate governance arrangements for sponsored public bodies were fit for purpose but did not lay down any general principles for determining whether they were.

Four Case Studies
Not many Scottish Parliament committee reports can be seen as relating to the accountability implications of quango structure, but four illustrations are set out below (see appendix at end of this chapter for report references).

An important initial quango report was on the Scottish Qualifications Agency (SQA) following the examination fiasco of 2000 when school examination results were delayed or issued erroneously, examined by both the enterprise and the education committees. The education committee recommended that 'the powers of the executive and ministers to intervene in the operation of SQA and the circumstances in which they may do so should be clarified and detailed' but did not identify the corporate status of the SQA as a major cause of the problems.

The enterprise committee report had the sharper focus on governance and its report is perhaps the major analytical contribution on quangos in the 10 years of the parliament. It found that the main issues in the SQA case were operational but that the governance arrangements, though typical for an NDPB, did not meet SQA's circumstances. It saw the 'potential for a closer relationship between ministers and NDPBs, whilst observing the important protocols of the arm's length nature of the relationship, for instance in decisions on awards' and asked more generally, post-devolution, 'to what extent should ministers be directly accountable for the arm's length bodies which they sponsor? Where should the line be drawn between aspects for which one could reasonably expect a minister to have direct responsibility, and those which lie beyond it? This is perhaps a matter which should be considered in due course by the parliament and the executive' – a call that remained unanswered.

Scottish Enterprise, created in 1991 to fund regeneration and training, has attracted frequent concern. In December 1999, the enterprise and lifelong learning committee issued interim conclusions on the delivery of local economic services stating that 'there is congestion within the field of local economic development services in Scotland. There is confusion, overlay, duplication and even active competition between the many agencies involved.' By 2006 the situation had barely changed as the network of local enterprise companies had been preserved after initial attempts to remove it; the audit committee had undertaken a special audit in 2004 after media criticism. Another report by the enterprise committee focused on the funding problems of Scottish Enterprise and was critical over the lack of early warning to ministers about budgetary problems and the application of resource accounting to asset-holding quangos – but it did not question the basic structure. It was the SNP government's decision in 2007 that reduced the number of local enterprise companies from 21 to six and transferred skills training to a new private company, Skills Development Scotland Ltd, which also took over Careers Scotland.

Communities Scotland was the national housing agency that was previously Scottish Homes (itself a merger of the Scottish Special Housing Association and the Scottish arm of the Housing Corporation). The Housing (Scotland) Act 2001 set up Communities Scotland as an agency within the Scottish executive.

The social justice committee's view on this loss of a statutory role was bland and brief: 'the committee welcomes the fact that the functions of the agency will now be open to scrutiny via ministerial accountability to parliament. The committee would welcome further details on how the minister proposes to separate the different roles of the agency and how to report its work to the parliament.' In 2007, it lost its agency status as well and without MSP scrutiny was abolished as a corporate entity, with its regulatory functions moving to the new Scottish Housing Regulator.

The Scottish Arts Council is the classic money-moving quango, with a high profile and a statutory role. Merging it with Scottish Screen, legally a triple play of registered charity, company limited by guarantee and non-departmental public body, to form Creative Scotland seemed like a bright idea and a simple matter of appointing a common board of directors and then passing legislation. Implementation of this has proved very difficult and the education and finance committees were drawn in. The latter was scathing on the transitional costs of the merger and the uncosted implications of potential redundancies of staff. The education and lifelong learning committee uncovered the extraordinary fact that ministers did not believe that they actually had needed to legislate to create the new body but otherwise followed the typical pattern of not addressing whether the corporate structure was appropriate to the task.

Conclusion

Writing about Scottish quangos in 1999, I suggested that a preservation of the inherited system was more likely than it might first appear because devolution was partly a response to innovation fatigue in public services. But I felt that there would be pressure for greater formal accountability and that the category most vulnerable to such pressures would be that of the funding body quango with a titularly private clientele – Scottish Homes and housing associations, Scottish Enterprise and Local Enterprise Companies (LECs), the Scottish Arts Council and its performing companies. In the event, none of these has survived intact. Scottish Homes is gone and housing association support taken within the Scottish government, not even as an agency. Scottish Enterprise (and Highland and Island Enterprise) survive but have lost their training and regeneration functions and their local networks. The Scottish Arts Council has lost its funding of the national companies back to the government, and is set for merger itself. In every case there has been some parliamentary investigation of the changes, but focusing on policy implication rather than structures.

I also felt that the parliamentary committees were 'likely to focus on the gap between spending power and accountability, and have a general preference for statutory governmental structures rather than local public spending bodies. The committees' investigations are likely to produce an accumulation of pressure and publicity that will make the use of quango mechanisms to conceal the size of the public sector a self-defeating process.' In some ways this has happened; quangos remain a term of abuse and when a particular one goes wrong (as with the SQA) there will be no shortage of scrutiny and blame. But there has not been a coherent line of criticism from the parliament about the structures of the public sector that will best promote its accountability tasks.

The arm's length aspects of quangos may give a greater public gain from transparency and publicity than any loss from distancing. Burying functions within government (both central and local) can allow complacency and inefficiency in the way that they are undertaken. It may be right that the parliament has been slow to advocate the re-incorporation of quangos in the name of better control by MSPs. Ministers have often used accountability arguments when justifying quango abolition, but they have their own reasons for seeking direct ministerial control. This may question the conventional wisdom that executives like quangos because they can distance them from direct accountability and are more efficient at regulatory oversight, while legislatures dislike them for this same lack of accountability.

This whole debate is all part of the fact that the Scottish Parliament was created from first principles but a Scottish government from inherited structures. Once the new structures were under way their life-blood is naturally politics, and it has become hard to separate out the context from the content. The parliament has been alert to its role on policy issues, but less so on its guardianship of the framework of public business. Perhaps the way forward is a Scottish Parliament public administration committee which, if its Westminster counterpart is anything to go by, might generate lively insights and debate and show that after 10 years the parliament was not afraid to borrow successful innovations from its older cousin.

Appendix: Committee reports cited

Audit Committee (2nd report 2003), *How Government Works in Scotland*, (5th report 2004), *Scottish Enterprise: Special Audit Examination*

Education Committee (11th report 2000), *Examination Results Inquiry*

Education, Lifelong Learning and Culture Committee (3rd report 2008), *Creative Scotland bill Stage 1*

Enterprise and Lifelong Learning Committee (6th report 2000), *Report on the Inquiry into the Governance of the Scottish Qualifications Agency*, (12th report 2004), *Stage 1 Report on the Further and Higher Education (Scotland) bill*, (11th report 2006), *Report on the Management of Budgets at Scottish Enterprise and the Proposed Restructuring of Enterprise Agencies*

Finance Committee (6 May 2008), *Report on Financial Memorandum of the Creative Scotland bill*

Procedures Committee (3rd report 2003), *The Founding Principles of the Scottish Parliament*

Social Justice Committee (1st report 2001), *Stage 1 Report on the Housing (Scotland) bill*

Chapter 19

The Scottish Parliament as seen from London

Peter Riddell

The Scottish Parliament has been largely ignored at the centre of UK politics in London. From 1999 until the formation of the SNP minority administration in spring 2007, most members of the House of Commons, and the London-based media, paid practically no attention to developments in Edinburgh. Even Scottish MPs, reduced in numbers after the redistribution at the 2005 general election, recognised that they were largely talking to themselves if they raised Scottish affairs, and knew that they had to concentrate on UK-level issues such as the economy, defence or foreign affairs if they wanted to advance their careers and make a wider political impact. There has been a devolution of attention, and knowledge, as well as of powers.

The main reason is that Scottish devolution has never been a real UK-wide issue. Despite the amount of constitutional legislation in the first Tony Blair term from 1997 until 2001, there was a broader reform agenda. Blair had little interest in constitutional issues, which he virtually never mentioned in any speeches or interviews. The Edinburgh parliament was designed by Scots, via the Scottish Constitutional Convention, with no input from the English political classes. For Scots, it was their creation and they did not want others to meddle.

For Blair – and Jack Straw, shadow home secretary in charge of the constitutional agenda after July 1994 – devolution was essentially a Scottish matter which had developed its own momentum. This was reinforced both by the powerful group of Scottish MPs among the Labour leadership in London and by a belief that delivering on the devolution pledge was a way of honouring John Smith's legacy. Blair and Straw were also concerned that any arrangements for Scotland should not have negative effects on the New Labour programme as a whole. In order to avoid repeating the time-consuming arguments at Westminster over the devolution legislation of the late 1970s, they were determined that, this time, any bill should not divert resources and attention from Blair's priorities to establish Labour as a party of government, and from his domestic reform agenda. As Blair put it privately, he did not want the tail of devolution to wag the dog of his New Labour government.

Blair's only major change to the devolution plans inherited from Smith was to insist that there should be a referendum in Scotland, and a separate one in Wales. In Scotland, there were separate questions on the principle and on tax varying powers. Scottish Labour supporters of devolution initially regarded this as a betrayal and a threat to their hopes for devolution. But, in the event, their fears proved to be misplaced. After Labour's landslide victory in May 1997 and the disappearance of Conservative MPs from Scotland (and Wales), the opponents of devolution were significantly weakened. There was largely token opposition as, first, the referendum legislation went through parliament, and, then, what became the Scotland Act 1998 was passed. These bills were considered on the floor of the Commons in thinly attended debates where almost the only non-Scottish speakers came from the Conservative benches (unavoidably since they had no Scottish MPs), and the lead was taken by Michael Ancram. He was a former Scottish Office minister who had lost his Edinburgh seat in 1987 and has represented Devizes since 1992. So, in practice, the referendum of September 1997 both legitimised and entrenched the creation of the Scottish Parliament. Even though it would be statutorily possible for the Westminster Parliament to repeal the Scotland Act, it would be impossible in practice without a further referendum in Scotland.

But Blair always thought of constitutional reform like ticking a box, to mark a commitment fulfilled. He took little interest in the practical arrangements over the legislation, and its implementation, which were overseen by Lord Irvine of Lairg as chairman of cabinet committees on the constitution. And after the legislation was passed in 1998, Blair hardly ever mentioned what was unquestionably one of the major achievements of his government. He left Scottish political issues to his many colleagues from Scottish constituencies, including Gordon Brown, Robin Cook, Donald Dewar, George Robertson and Alistair Darling. He did not want to invest time, or energy, in the often bitter internal disputes of the Scottish Labour Party.

That disinclination to be involved in Scottish affairs was shared by most other ministers and Labour MPs, as well as by the other parties. The Liberal Democrats' Scottish party was anyway semi-autonomous within a federal structure, while the Scottish Conservatives accepted that any revival in Scotland would be best achieved there and that the English party could do little to help. The underlying assumption was to accept the logic of devolution: that Scottish affairs should be left to the Scots.

That process of ghettoisation was reinforced by changes in media behaviour. The always close, if often abrasive, relationship between the Scottish media and political classes became even closer after devolution. The main Scottish newspapers and broadcasters focused on developments in the Edinburgh parliament, and reduced their coverage of events at Westminster. The mirror image was a reduction in Scottish coverage by London-based newspapers and broadcasters. A common view was that arguments in the Scottish Parliament were only of interest to Scottish readers and viewers and not those in England. So stories which appeared in the Scottish editions of national newspapers, or on specifically Scottish news and current affairs programmes, generally did not appear in English editions. Readers in London can find out more about politics in Spain or Australia than about politics a few hundred miles to their north in Scotland.

So there was widespread ignorance in London, amongst politicians, civil servants and journalists, about what was happening in Edinburgh. This applied not just to political squabbles (who was up and down) but also to policy developments and innovations in the way the parliament operated. There was much more interchange and swapping of experiences between Edinburgh, Cardiff and Belfast than between any of these devolved capitals and London. I found from my experience chairing the advisory board of the Economic and Social Research Council programme on devolution and constitutional change that it was almost impossible to generate any interest from London-based journalists and politicians. There was practically no interest at Westminster in, for example, the new committee structure in Edinburgh (combining select committees and what are now called at Westminster public bill committees), the creation of a business committee to control what happens in the chamber, and a new and more open system of petitions. It took nearly a decade for the House of Commons to take up, in a very cautious and hesitant way, the Scottish procedures on e-petitions. The Lords constitution committee was rare in 2002 in looking at lessons for Westminster from Holyrood, Cardiff Bay and Stormont: highlighting, in particular, the use of pre-legislative scrutiny.

The increasing policy divergence between the politics of Tony Blair's government in London and the Labour-led administrations in Edinburgh, as well as Cardiff, always attracted surprisingly little attention at Westminster. Blair himself was irritated by this divergence, notably during the negotiations on abolition of up-front tuition fees which dominated the coalition-making process of Scottish Labour with the Liberal Democrats following the first Scottish Parliament elections in 1999. He reportedly remarked that he would not have backed devolution if he had realised that the result would be such policy differences. But, then, Blair was never really a pluralist. However, towards the end of his premiership, he liked to highlight improvements in, say, NHS outcomes, and reductions in waiting lists, in England compared with what he claimed was the lack of progress in health outcomes in the devolved administrations.

The widely discussed phenomenon of post-code lotteries – differing outcomes and standards of social and welfare provision in England – was barely noted in public debate when the Scottish government has adopted different policies, for example on tuition fees and elderly care. There was some grumbling from Conservative MPs about unfair treatment and about a more generous financial settlement in Scotland than in England – in terms of public spending per head. This was portrayed as the result of the Barnett formula allocating the main grant from the Treasury to the devolved administrations. (This is an area of considerable controversy, not least because many of the allegations about higher public spending per head in Scotland do not take account of greater needs because of social deprivation, and they tend to over-simplify the Barnett formula.) But for most of this period, the English question/English backlash was more discussed than apparent. There is no evidence of resentment against Scotland playing any measurable part in either the 2001 or 2005 general elections.

The lack of interest at Westminster was, paradoxically, underpinned by the political closeness between ministers in Edinburgh and London. As long as Labour was in power at Westminster and dominated the coalition in Edinburgh, there were in-built forces to minimise and keep out of public view any differences and tensions (some of which, especially on care for the elderly, led to stinging private rows). Successive Labour First Ministers could easily ring up a minister in London, whom they generally knew well. In particular, the presence of Gordon Brown at the Treasury throughout this period ensured that any financial difficulties could be smoothed out.

A crucial factor also was that, from 2000 until 2008, public spending was rising sharply in real, inflated adjusted terms, and this gave the Scottish administration scope to pursue its distinctive policies on higher education and elderly care without squeezing other programmes.

However, the absence of problems was conditional upon broad harmony between the leaderships in Edinburgh and London (despite the periodic private bust-ups), upon a benign economic and fiscal environment, and upon no real challenges to the intergovernmental arrangements. The elaborate mechanisms set up both in the original 1999 Scotland Act and informally via various concordats between the Scottish executive and Whitehall departments, were not really tested.

In other countries, either those with formal federal structures or even asymmetrical multi-level governments, disputes between the centre and devolved administrations have been routine. In Spain and Canada, these differences have led to lengthy legal challenges and constitutional debates. But none of this occurred in the UK during the first two terms of the Scottish Parliament. Common political and electoral interests smoothed over problems with both ministers and civil servants being very active behind the scenes to avoid open disputes. After all, the officials in the Scottish executive had previously served in the Scottish Office as part of a unified executive and they remained part of single national civil service, in theory at least.

These factors all contributed to what Lord Wilson of Dinton, cabinet secretary from early 1998 until summer 2002, when devolution was being established, described as the tendency of the British people 'to ignore big constitutional change. They behave like a patient who submits to surgery under anaesthetic, but only considers whether he wants the operation some time later when he begins to feel the consequences.' But the patient was given a sharp wake-up call in May 2007 when the SNP narrowly became the largest single group in the parliament, albeit just one seat ahead of Labour, and well short of an overall majority. Nonetheless, with Labour having lost several MSPs, the initiative lay with Alex Salmond, the SNP leader.

Salmond was, and remains, by far the best known SNP member in London. His effectiveness as a parliamentary performer elevated him above other Scottish politicians – not least through his ability to get under Gordon Brown's skin. He has put both the SNP and the Scottish Parliament on the map at Westminster.

Differences in political control in London and Edinburgh have also exposed the limitations of the informal understandings which underpinned devolution over its first eight years. The SNP administration has blamed London for not providing enough money – and these complaints are likely to increase as the growth of public spending is squeezed even more over the coming years. And there have also been disputes on specific policy areas, with both sides exaggerating differences.

So for Westminster politicians, Scotland has moved from being forgotten to being a problem. On the Labour side, and particularly for Brown, the SNP administration is a headache, an irritant and a challenge. For the Conservatives, the reality of a more assertive Scotland has revived – reignited would be too strong a term – debate about the alleged unfairness of the 1999 legislation: in short, the English question. The Tories' democracy task force, chaired by Kenneth Clarke, argued that current arrangements 'represent a long-term threat to the integrity of the Union. They do so because they create an imbalance in the ability of the different nations of the UK to make their own laws and to protect their own interests. We believe that, if this problem is not addressed, the resulting sense of grievance on the part of the Union's largest nation, the English, could undermine the current constitutional settlement.' This is the familiar West Lothian question: the ability of Scottish MPs at Westminster to vote on legislation primarily affecting the English, when neither they, nor, of course, English MPs had any say in voting on legislative matters devolved to Holyrood. This might become an acute matter if any government lost its majority amongst English MPs but could carry legislation at Westminster affecting English constituents thanks to the votes of Scottish MPs. In practice, this would only arise with a Labour government either with a very small majority in the Commons or if it was the largest party in a hung parliament. This dilemma would not apply if the Tories had a majority or were the largest single party.

This argument has focused on two aspects: one constitutional and the other financial. The Tories have sought to make the asymmetrical arrangements more symmetrical. But this is very difficult for the simple reason that England makes up more than four-fifths of the UK. In the absence of elected regional government in England – for which there is little apparent demand following its rejection by north-east voters in November 2004 – proposals for an English parliament or English votes for English laws (excluding Scottish and presumably Welsh and Northern Ireland MPs from voting on specifically English issues) risk destabilising the whole union. Leaving aside procedural and technical difficulties, there is the inherent problem that decisions on English legislation are bound to have knock-on effects in the other nations. But Scots and other MPs will not have a say. The Tories have been split between the desire of most, including David Cameron, to preserve the Union and their search for a workable compromise. The democracy task force proposed having English-only committee and report stages for English measures but allowing all MPs to vote on second and third readings. This would still involve considerable practical problems, including the implications of any revised House of Commons procedure for the currently appointed House of Lords; as long as the second chamber is not elected from territorial constituencies, it would be difficult to apply English-only stages as suggested for the Commons.

The most recent British Social Attitudes survey in January 2009 showed an increase from 22% to 32% since 2003 in the number of people in England feeling that Scotland gets more than its fair share of government spending. (A consistent three-fifths agree that Scottish MPs should not vote on English legislation.) But there is little other evidence that the English resent Scottish and Welsh devolution. The English backlash is limited because a majority feel that devolution has not made much difference to the way the UK is governed.

In the short-term, the main focus has been financial with a special Lords committee investigating the Barnett formula. But most important of all is that the fiscal and spending environment is certain to change sharply from the first 10 years of Scottish devolution. The economic crisis means that overall growth in public spending will slow very sharply and this will squeeze the central grant to Scotland as well as to other spending programmes. That will test the devolution settlement as much, if not more, than arguments over the balance of constitutional arrangements. A newly-elected David Cameron government would face little immediate pressure to tackle the English question since this would not be a problem for the Tories if they had a Commons majority. A much more pressing priority would be sorting out UK public finances – and managing their consequences for devolution in Scotland.

Chapter 20

Opening Doors: Devolution in Wales and the Scottish Parliament, 1999–2009

Alan Trench

Even before it came into being, the Scottish Parliament played an important role in Wales's devolution debates. The recognition of the distinctiveness of an historic nation within the United Kingdom by establishing a devolved legislature with a wide range of powers was a potent symbol and rallying-point for advocates of devolution in Wales. That was not all; Scotland's ability to debate seriously the form devolution should take through the 1990s helped shape debates in Wales about whether devolution should happen and the form it should take. Because devolved self-government was clearly a project of the unionist parties and operated in a UK context, the Scottish debates also enabled proponents of devolution to counter arguments that devolution was part of a slippery slope toward separatism, which had long been used by its opponents in Wales.

In contrast to Scotland, where the Scottish Constitutional Convention articulated and made manifest the range of support for devolution and enabled the political parties to resolve questions about the form it should take, Wales's form of devolution was very largely developed within the Labour Party. What Labour embraced and offered the public at the 1997 referendum was effectively a democratised version of the secretary of state for Wales – three ministers were to be replaced by 60 Assembly members. It gained only limited support from civil society (which in any case is weak compared with Scotland), and received a less-than-ringing endorsement at the 1997 referendum – securing the support of less than 51% of the voters and a winning margin of some 7,000 votes. In this context, describing devolution as the 'settled will' of the people of Wales (as John Smith did for Scotland) would have invited derision. By saying devolution was a process not an event, Ron Davies (secretary of state for Wales 1997-98) made the boldest claim that credibly he could.

The Assembly was only to have powers of making delegated legislation, and to exercise them as a single body in law, more like a local council than an elected legislature. The progress of devolution in Wales has been much more uncertain and faltering than in Scotland, and has involved a constant process of constitutional development and debate, which has gone on in tandem with the process of the people of Wales trying to work out what sort of a nation they are and what their nationhood should mean in institutional terms.

In this chapter I shall suggest that the importance of the Scottish Parliament for devolution in Wales has been two-fold; it has served as an example of what democratic devolved government can look like, both in general and in some detailed respects, and it has opened the door to wider possibilities for the development of devolution in Wales. Perhaps the most important point, though, is that the existence and nature of the Scottish Parliament have been the focus of much debate about devolution in Wales, in a way that is not reciprocated or paralleled in Scotland or elsewhere. Those involved in devolution in Wales regularly look to what happens in Scotland as an example and a model, rather than simply looking to factors within Wales; in Scotland, reference to Wales in thinking about the performance and direction of devolution is vanishingly rare.

The Richard Commission and the 'Scottish Model'
The institutionally weak form of devolution in Wales has meant that there has been an ongoing constitutional debate, more or less constantly since 1999, about the nature, form and powers of the devolved institutions. Within a couple of years of its establishment, an internal *Assembly Review of Procedure* recommended a greater separation between the deliberative and executive sides of the Assembly, effected informally with the naming of the executive as the 'Welsh Assembly Government' in April 2002 and the increasing creation of separate staff and other resources for elected members on the parliamentary side of the Assembly.

However, the most important changes stem from the report of the Richard Commission, or formally the Commission on the Powers and Electoral Arrangements of the National Assembly, set up under the 2002 coalition agreement between Labour and the Liberal Democrats. Its report, published in April 2004, was a landmark in thinking about devolution for Wales, and was the most dramatic use yet of the 'Scottish model' in Wales (Commission on Powers and Electoral Arrangements 2004). In many ways, the commission was a substitute for the constitutional convention Wales never had; its membership came from all the political parties in the National Assembly, with a large number of non-party members appointed following an open advertisement, and it took evidence at meetings, orally and in writing from across Wales. Lord Richard was keen after the report was published to emphasise it was 'evidence led', and the fact that it was produced by a group of people with wide experience of public life who reflected over an extended period on the problems of devolved government, without being directly subject to party political concerns, may account for the report's apparent radicalism. In place of bargains struck within the Labour Party, the Richard Commission took a synoptic view. The report discussed in some detail the status quo and possible ways of extending devolution, such as a 'Northern Ireland' model where some powers are devolved outright and others are matters on which the Assembly can legislate with the assent of the UK government, and which the UK government could transfer to the devolved legislature by secondary legislation. But what the commission recommended looked very like the model of devolution enacted for Scotland in 1998. That recommendation was for:

- An Assembly with general legislative powers – that is, one able to legislate for all matters save those expressly reserved to Westminster (though the list of reservations it contemplated would have included the legal system, policing and criminal justice), with effect from 2011
- A separate executive, accountable to the Assembly
- An increase in the number of Assembly members to 80, and the use of the single transferable vote (STV) system to elect them
- A transitional process for the acquisition of powers before 2011, by the grant of increased powers by Westminster Acts of Parliament

The recommended use of STV was one of the most controversial of the proposals and one that departed most radically from arrangements in Scotland. It was rendered necessary by electoral reality; the problem of increasing membership of the Assembly when there were only 40 Westminster seats in Wales. (Historically, Wales has been less generously represented at Westminster than Scotland, though it is still represented more generously than England is.) Otherwise, though, the recommendations mirrored what had already happened in Scotland.

While welcomed by many non-party political observers (and a number of political parties, notably Plaid Cymru), these recommendations crucially drew only limited support from within the Labour Party. Within days of the report's publication, First Minister Rhodri Morgan had distanced the Labour Party from the recommendations about the electoral system, for example. Before six months had passed since publication, at a special conference in September 2004, Welsh Labour rejected most of the key provisions of the report and adopted a paper called *Better Governance for Wales* – which, not by coincidence, was the name of the UK government's June 2005 white paper setting out the proposals which were then enacted in the Government of Wales Act 2006.

Apart from separating the executive from the legislature (a matter on which all parties in Wales, and everyone involved in the work of the National Assembly, were agreed), the 2006 Act model is a long way away from the Richard Commission blueprint. It creates lengthy and convoluted processes for conferring legislative powers on the National Assembly, using various different routes and creating cumbersome procedures between the two governments and Westminster and Cardiff Bay to consider what are known as 'legislative competence orders'. A constitutional lawyer can see a Scottish influence here too, with the various order-making powers in the Scotland Act 1998 that give vital flexibility to the Scottish arrangements if the UK and Scottish governments and parliaments can agree – but for Wales they are elevated from a convenient behind-the-scenes device to a crucial constitutional mechanism. The Act also provides for the Assembly to acquire what the white paper calls 'primary legislative powers' – and what in popular debate are often, wrongly, called Scottish-style legislative powers – but only after a referendum approves this. Calling a referendum needs the approval of five separate veto players, though, and in any case, the 2006 Act leaves the number of Assembly Members at 60. The Act also did not alter the existing electoral system (which is not very proportional, and significantly advantages the Labour Party), save for banning candidates running for both constituency seats and on the regional list – a move which prompted widespread criticism not just from the other political parties, but also from many academic observers and the Electoral Commission.

Is the Scottish Parliament a Model for Wales?

It is worth asking why the Scottish Parliament is an attractive model for Wales. It is easy to see Wales as Scotland's backward Celtic cousin, with more limited institutions and sense of itself, a greater degree of dominance by England, which is keen to follow in the footsteps of its older relation as soon as it can. Many observers do so, and even a number of academic students of devolution fail to engage with Wales seriously or understand the questions devolution raises from a Welsh perspective. And there are a large number of similarities. Each country strongly rejected the Conservatives during their long period in office from 1979 to 1997, and so found itself governed by a Tory secretary of state whose local mandate was weak. In both countries, the Labour Party has long been dominant, and continues to regard itself as the naturally dominant party. Each country also has long-standing local bastions of Labour dominance, whether it be Glasgow or the Rhondda Valley. Within each Labour Party there are deep divisions about how far devolution should go (though few in Scotland would go as far as a number of Welsh MPs privately do in wishing to abolish the National Assembly). The fact that Wales has comparatively few institutions manifesting its nationhood – no separate legal or banking system, no separate established religion – helps to fuel the argument that Wales is Scotland writ small.

There are some key differences, however. One is the geographic divisions between north, south and mid Wales, and their strong transport and economic ties to England (and to different parts of England). A second is language, and the distinct cultural life that comes with it (but also the divisions between Welsh-speakers and non-Welsh-speakers). Another has been the historic ambivalence of Plaid Cymru about its long-term aspirations – whether it seeks 'independence' and what independence in this context would mean. But most important has been what comes out of all those divisions. For the most part, the people of Wales (of whatever background) know that they are Welsh, and that this makes them different from the English. Cultural nationhood is a well-established factor, and due to the increasing use of the Welsh language since the 1980s this has become a more developed feature of life in Wales. However, what that cultural identity means in constitutional or political terms is much less clear. It is one thing to sing 'Cwm Rhondda' or enjoy the humour of Max Boyce. It is another to form a distinctive society or political community.

The last 12 years or so, since the referendum campaign and then the establishment of the National Assembly, have therefore been a period during which that process of considering and debating Wales's constitutional future has taken place. It has been a slow and confusing process, and often one carried out by a political elite with little regard to what the general public wants (as most notably exemplified by the process of bargaining that produced the Government of Wales Act 2006). Nonetheless, the process has gone on and, as Table 1 shows, a general consensus for devolution has emerged, probably in an extended form to its present one – what in shorthand is called a 'parliament' with law-making powers rather than an 'assembly' with only executive ones.

Table 1: Constitutional Preferences in Wales 1997-2007						
Constitutional Preference: Wales should...	*1997*	*1999*	*2001*	*2003*	*2006*	*2007*
Be independent, separate from UK and EU or separate from UK but part of EU	14.1	9.6	12.3	13.9	11.5	12.2
Remain part of the UK with its own elected parliament which has some law-making and taxation powers	19.6	29.9	38.8	37.8	42.1	43.8
Remain part of the UK with its own elected Assembly which has limited law making powers only	26.8	35.3	25.5	27.1	25.0	27.5
Remain part of the UK without an elected Assembly	39.5	25.3	24.0	21.2	21.3	16.5

Source: *Wales Devolution Monitoring Report, January 2008* (London: The Constitution Unit, 2008), p. 68, available at www.ucl.ac.uk/constitution-unit/research/devolution/MonReps/Wales_Jan08.pdf

This pattern of opinion is confirmed by a number of commercial polls asking what choice voters would make in a referendum to bring in the 'primary legislative powers' set out in Part 4 of the 2006 Act, of which the most recent showed both 52% would support wider powers, and 39% oppose it (BBC News 2009). In this sense, Ron Davies's 'process' has led to an emergent consensus about what devolution should mean, and one where public opinion is ahead of institutional actuality; that Wales should have a strong form of self-government within the United Kingdom.

But the crablike process of moving toward a more stable settlement continues. The coalition between Labour and Plaid Cymru in May 2007 resulted in both a commitment to hold a referendum on primary legislative powers before the next Assembly elections in 2011, and to set up a constitutional convention – the All Wales Convention, chaired by a former UK Ambassador to the United

Nations, Sir Emyr Jones Parry – to advise on issues relating to that referendum. The role of the Convention is unclear though; it treats itself as a neutral advisory body deliberating on the merits of a referendum, while both the BBC and the emergent 'no' campaign regard the Convention as a government-funded 'yes' campaign. In any case, the passage of time and opposition to an early referendum from some key politicians (including former UK Welsh secretary Peter Hain and Assembly Presiding Officer Dafydd Elis-Thomas) mean that a referendum before 2012 looks increasingly unlikely.

What is the importance of the Scottish Parliament here? A more nuanced explanation than 'Wales follows where Scotland leads' is that Scotland opens doors to what is possible within the United Kingdom and that Wales is then able to consider how to use the opportunities that arise as a result. What use Wales makes of those opportunities, and whether it wants to use them at all, is a matter that is open for debate. Without those doors being open, it is questionable whether Wales would be able to take those steps. It was no accident that the Welsh referendum in 1997 was held a week after the Scottish one, in the belief that the widely-expected 'yes' vote in Scotland would boost support in Wales. In each case, it is decisions and developments in Wales that have been key to deciding what happens, reflecting Welsh conditions rather than a straightforward determinism of aping Scotland.

Chapter 21

The Scottish Parliament, Constitutional Change and the UK's Haphazard Union[1]

Charlie Jeffery

The Scottish Parliament is here to stay. With very few exceptions such as Tam Dalyell and Michael Forsyth almost no-one any more calls for its abolition. The main opponents of devolution in the 1997 referendum campaigns – the Conservative Party and parts of the business community – are now fully reconciled to the existence of, and to working through, the parliament. In public opinion there is only a residual 10% or so who favour a return to direct rule by UK government. This does not mean that the current situation represents the 'settled will' of the Scottish people. The question of how Scotland and the Scots should be governed remains open. In one sense that is inevitable, given the commitment of the SNP to Scottish independence, and the union vs. independence debate it perpetuates in Scottish politics.

But in many respects the SNP played down the constitutional question once the Scottish Parliament was established. At all the Scottish Parliament elections so far the SNP sought above all to present an image of greater competence to govern than its main competitor, Labour. Only when it had entered government in 2007 did the SNP put the constitutional question in the foreground, publishing a white paper on Scotland's constitutional options in August 2007 and launching a consultative 'national conversation' on those options.

Where there was constitutional discussion before 2007, it was mainly of two kinds: anti-SNP electoral tactic, especially on the part of Labour, which periodically (and most fiercely in 2007) conjured up scare stories about what independence might mean to prevent the erosion of its support by the SNP; or a rather more subtle background hum on the adequacy of the devolution arrangements, and in particular the funding of devolution. Back in the first session of the Scottish Parliament (1999-2003) a number of figures in the SNP worked to prompt a debate (largely outside the parliament) on fiscal autonomy, which has gradually opened out and become a mainstream and cross-party concern. The funding of devolution was, for example, the dominant theme in the 2006 report of the Liberal Democrats' Steel Commission, *Moving to Federalism – A New Settlement for Scotland*, in March 2006. And, more broadly, in the period 2003–07 there was an increasingly vigorous debate – mainly among think tanks and academics

[1] This chapter was informed by the papers presented to, and discussion at, the James Madison Trust seminar series on Constitutional Scenarios at the University of Edinburgh in autumn 2008.

– about how the money the parliament spends should be financed. The dominant theme has been that the parliament should itself raise more (and in some views all) of what it spends: to improve its accountability to the Scottish electorate; to introduce tougher disciplines into spending decisions; or simply as a next stage of devolution.

Almost entirely absent from constitutional debate, before and after 2007, has been a discussion of how the parliament works. Unlike in Wales, where many of the reforms debated and introduced since 1997 have been about the structure and effectiveness of the National Assembly as a decision-making body, the way the parliament operates has not been the issue. The issue has been what it can and should be able to do.

Choosing Scotland's Future
That issue was inevitably highlighted when the SNP entered government in 2007. The SNP's constitutional white paper, *Choosing Scotland's Future* was published in August 2007. It set out the SNP's constitutional preference – independence – and a possible route to it: a referendum tentatively scheduled for 2010 which, if won, would empower the Scottish government to negotiate with the UK government on the terms of Scottish independence. Voices in all of the three unionist parties in the Scottish Parliament (Labour, the Conservatives and the Liberal Democrats) have at times supported having a referendum, most prominently in the then Labour leader, Wendy Alexander's challenge in May 2008 to 'bring it on'. But more recently the unionist parties appear to have unified on an anti-referendum position. As they together have a majority in the parliament that, it would seem, is that.

Except that it is not. The SNP government's white paper also set out – at rather greater length than its vision of Scottish independence – possibilities for devolving additional powers to the Scottish Parliament within the UK. The white paper did not say much about financing the parliament. But since then – partly in an argument about Scotland's scope to respond to the current economic crisis, partly in an attempt to influence the unionist variant of the constitutional debate – the government has clarified its position. It is essentially the same as that on legislative powers: the SNP favours full fiscal autonomy in an independent Scotland, but in the interim would also support what it calls 'devolution-max' – maximum fiscal autonomy within the UK, that is the right to set tax rates, define tax bases and raise money through borrowing – as the next-best alternative.

This duality of preference for independence *and* openness to further devolution is now something of an SNP mantra. It is significant for two reasons. First it signals an understanding in the SNP that 'independence' is not an absolute and that there may ultimately be little practical distinction between 'devolution-max' within the UK and notional independence in a British Isles/European

Union setting in which there would still be extensive interdependences and commonalities across a Scottish-UK border.

Second it sets out a terrain of further devolution which overlaps with unionist thinking, and draws the unionist parties onto SNP turf. This was confirmed in the unionist response to the SNP white paper. The central figure was the then Scottish Labour leader Wendy Alexander. In a speech in November 2007 she both set out her vision for constitutional reform, and trailed the establishment of a unionist commission on devolution which had been agreed in complex hexagonal negotiations between Labour, the Conservatives and the Liberal Democrats in the Scottish Parliament, and their Westminster counterparts. Alexander's vision was distinctive. She signalled an openness to further devolution of powers, and gave particular attention to strengthening the fiscal accountability of the Scottish Parliament through additional fiscal autonomy. But she also embedded that advocacy of fuller devolution in a vision of stronger union, emphasising the benefits of sharing risk across the UK as a way of guaranteeing a single, UK-wide 'social citizenship'.

With that speech Alexander set out the kernel of a unionist argument in which support for fuller devolution could be balanced by more systematic consideration of the meaning and terms of union. However, she resigned seven months later over a campaign donation controversy. Her successor as Scottish Labour leader, Iain Gray, has shown rather less interest in the constitutional question. The commission she trailed was set up in April 2008 as the Commission on Scottish Devolution, chaired by Sir Kenneth Calman and with the imprimatur of the Scottish and UK variants of the unionist parties (and, initially at least, without input from the SNP). The commission to an extent has pursued Alexander's vision, stressing in its December 2008 interim report a number of fundamental 'principles of union' as the context for a discussion of the adequacy of the powers and financial arrangements of the Scottish Parliament and of the intergovernmental relations linking it to Westminster and Whitehall. A best guess of the direction its final report is headed is one of recommending modest enhancements of current legislative powers and a widening of the current scope of fiscal autonomy, including borrowing powers.

Such recommendations would be uncontroversial in Scotland, or perhaps even judged as a bare minimum of what is desirable. That is not the case in Westminster, where there is both limited understanding of the current dynamics of Scottish politics and substantial residual antipathy to devolution in parts of both the Labour and Conservative parties. These differences within the unionist camp suggest the Calman Commission will find it difficult to win a general endorsement both in Scotland and Westminster. There is a stark contrast between the difficulty there will be in establishing a single cross-party, cross-border, unionist position on the future powers of the Scottish Parliament and the simplicity of the SNP's message: independence if we can, more devolution if we can't. That message seems set to remain the benchmark for the constitutional debate in Scotland, and to continue to set its agenda.

It does so not just because of party political dynamics, but also public opinion. The SNP agenda maps neatly onto the centre of gravity of Scottish public opinion. The most reliable measure of Scottish opinion is the Scottish Social Attitudes survey, which has now built up an impressive data set. This shows *inter alia*:

- That devolution is the most popular constitutional option of the Scots, and usually a majority option, while independence is consistently favoured by a significant minority and the abolition of devolution by a small minority (Table 1)
- That 60%-plus of Scots think the Scottish Parliament should have more powers and that 50%-plus think it should have power to raise its own resources to cover its spending (Table 2)

Table 1: Scotland's Constitutional Options									
Scotland should ...	1999	2000	2001	2002	2003	2004	2005	2006	2007
Be independent	28	30	27	30	26	32	35	30	23
Remain part of the UK with its own elected Parliament	58	55	60	52	55	45	44	54	63
Remain part of the UK without an elected Parliament	10	12	9	12	13	17	14	9	10

These data show that further-reaching devolution is – and is consistently – the default option in Scottish public opinion. They show that the Scottish will may indeed be settled – but not on the status quo. This pattern of public opinion at the very least sets a permissive context for further devolution, opening the door for a move at some point towards 'devolution-max'.

Table 2: More Powers for the Scottish Parliament?		'The Scottish Parliament should be given more powers'	'Now that Scotland has its own Parliament, it should pay for its services out of taxes collected in Scotland'
2001	Agree	68	52
	Neither	14	18
	Disagree	17	28
2003	Agree	59	51
	Neither	18	16
	Disagree	23	29
2007	Agree	66	57
	Neither	16	15
	Disagree	17	24

Scotland in the UK

There is a wider point to draw from the Scottish constitutional debate. Given that we are unlikely to see an independence referendum any time soon, whatever additional powers the Scottish Parliament might gain will be gained within the UK. But the Scottish constitutional debate, in both its unionist and nationalist variants is territorially narrow. The SNP by definition has a frame of reference limited to Scotland and focused on loosening Scotland's relationship with the rest of the UK. And though unionist perspectives typically have a UK dimension, they are always focused narrowly on Scotland's relationship with UK-level institutions. They generally do not consider the other component parts of the UK, Scotland's relation to them, or the implications of ideas on constitutional change in Scotland for the rest of the UK. So while the Steel Commission report had a title suggestive of UK-wide thinking – *Moving towards Federalism*, it had little of substance to say about what 'federalism' might mean in practice in Wales, Northern Ireland or England. Likewise the Calman Commission's focus on union – either at the level of general principles or focused on inter-governmental relations – is presented as an issue of the *bi*lateral relationship between Scottish and UK institutions. Mentions of the Northern Ireland Assembly, National Assembly for Wales, governing arrangements for England or of the people of Northern Ireland, England and Wales are either absent or incidental.

Perhaps even more significantly, the constitutional debate in Scotland in all its variants appears blind to the possible implications *for Scotland* of constitutional discussions about other parts of the UK. There are currently, in addition to the national conversation and the Calman Commission, three other forums for constitutional debate under way in the UK: an All-Wales Convention charged with preparing the ground for full, legislative devolution in Wales; an Independent Commission on Funding and Finance for Wales focused on how the National Assembly should be funded; and a House of Lords inquiry on the Barnett Formula. In addition, there have been substantial debates in the Conservative Party about how better to reflect English interests in Westminster legislation following devolution. Any or all of these debates could prompt changes of real and possibly immense significance to Scotland. Given England's size and the continued ability that brings even after devolution (and one suspects also even if Scotland were independent) to influence public debate and policy choices in Scotland, whatever happens to the government of England will bring spillovers into Scotland. And any changes to the system of financing devolution, possibly driven by prompts from Wales, possibly by the House of Lords committee inquiry into the Barnett formula, will also have implications for Scotland, perhaps setting constraints around the scope for Scottish fiscal autonomy.

It appears unlikely that these connectivities across jurisdictions and their implications will be considered systematically. To be blunt, they never have been. Before devolution there was no systematic view in central government across the special systems of territorial administration that evolved in Scotland, Wales and Northern Ireland. The devolution reforms themselves were not considered as a package, but as discrete reforms, each rebalancing the relationship of one part of the UK with the UK centre. And since devolution neither central government nor the devolved governments have sought to establish anything that might be called a system for the coordination of government across the UK as a whole, preferring an ad hoc and disconnected, bilateral approach. The UK has always been, and continues to be, a haphazard union, with an unordered, random quality. That creates very open-ended opportunities for any one component, like Scotland, to reshape its relationship to the union as a whole, perhaps even to leave it. But it also understates the interdependencies, and the scope for perhaps unwelcome spillovers, between jurisdictions as relationships are reshaped. As the debate on the future powers of the Scottish Parliament unfolds, its protagonists might do well to look up, see what is happening elsewhere in the UK, and understand better what it might mean for Scotland.

Selected Bibliography

D. Arter (2004), *The Scottish Parliament: A Scandinavian Style Assembly?* (London: Frank Cass).

D. Arter (2004), 'The Scottish Parliament and the Goal of a "New Politics": A Verdict on the First Four Years', at www.essex.ac.uk/ECPR/standinggroups/parliaments/papers/arter.pdf.

F. Bechhofer & D. McCrone (eds) (2009 forthcoming), *National Identity, Nationalism and Constitutional Change* (London: Palgrave).

N. Blain & D. Hutchison (eds) (2008), *The Media In Scotland* (Edinburgh: Edinburgh University Press).

C. Bromley, J. Curtice & L. Given (2007), *Attitudes to Discrimination in Scotland: 2006 Scottish Social Attitudes Survey* (Edinburgh: Scottish Government Social Research).

C. Bromley, J. Curtice, D. McCrone & A. Park (eds) (2006), *Has Devolution Delivered?* (Edinburgh: Edinburgh University Press).

A. Brown (2000), 'Designing the Scottish Parliament', *Parliamentary Affairs*, Vol. 53, pp. 542–556.

P. Cairney (2008), 'Has Devolution Changed the British Policy Style?, *British Politics*, 3, 3, pp. 350-72.

C.J. Carman (2006), *The Assessment of the Scottish Parliament's Public Petitions System 1999-2006.* Commissioned by the Scottish Parliament Information Centre for the Public Petitions Committee (SP Paper 654), available at: www.scottish.parliament.uk/business/committees/petitions/reports-06/pur06-PPS-assessment-01.htm

C.J. Carman, J. Mitchell & R. Johns (2008), 'The Unfortunate Natural Experiment in Ballot Design: The Scottish Parliamentary Elections of 2007', *Electoral Studies*, Vol. 27, pp. 442-59.

Commission on Scottish Devolution (2008), *The Future of Scottish Devolution within the Union*, at www.commissiononscottishdevolution.org.uk/uploads/2008-12-01-vol-1-final--bm.pdf.

Commission on Boundary Differences and Voting Systems (2006), *Putting Citizens First: Boundaries, Voting and Representation in Scotland* (Edinburgh: The Stationery Office).

Commission on the Powers and Electoral Arrangements of the National Assembly for Wales (2004), *Report of the Richard Commission* (Cardiff: National Assembly for Wales).

Consultative Steering Group (1999), *Shaping Scotland's Parliament: Report of the Consultative Steering Group on the Scottish Parliament: Presented to the Secretary of State for Scotland December 1998* (Edinburgh: Scottish Office), available at: www.scotland.gov.uk/library/documents-w5/rcsg-00.htm.

B. Crick & D. Millar (1995), *To Make the Parliament of Scotland a Model for Democracy* (Edinburgh: John Wheatley Centre).

J. Curtice (2007), 'Public Attitudes and Elections', Scotland Devolution Monitoring Report, May 2008, at www-server.bcc.ac.uk/constitution-unit/files/research/devolution/dmr/Scotland_Jan08.pdf.

J. Curtice, D. McCrone, N. McEwen, M. Marsh & R. Ormston (2009 forthcoming), *Revolution or Evolution? The 2007 Scottish Elections* (Edinburgh: Edinburgh University Press).

J. Curtice & B. Seyd (eds) (2009), *Has Devolution Worked?* (Manchester: Manchester University Press).

D. Farrell (2001), *Electoral Systems: A Comparative Introduction* (Houndmills: Palgrave).

R. Gould (2007), Independent Review of the Scottish Parliamentary and Local Government Elections 3 May 2007, available at www.electoralcommission.org.uk/document-summary?assetid=13223.

D. Halpin & G. Baxter (2008), 'Searching for "Tartan" Policy Bandwagons: Mapping the Mobilization of Organized Interests in Public Policy', paper given at Annual Meeting of the American Political Science Association, 28-31 August.

D. Halpin & G. Baxter (2008), 'Organised Interests in Scottish Public Policy: Questionnaire Survey Results', Project Report available at www.organisedinterests.co.uk/darrenhalpin/mobilisation.htm.

A. Herman (2002), *Scottish Englightenment: The Scots Invention of the Modern World* (London: Fourth Estate).

C.M.G. Himsworth & C.M. O'Neill (2003), *Scotland's Constitution: Law and Practice* (Edinburgh: Tottel Publishing).

House of Commons Modernisation Committee (1997–98), First Report, HC 190.

R. Johns, D. Denver, J. Mitchell & C. Pattie (2010 forthcoming), *Voting for a Scottish Government: the Scottish Parliament Election of 2007* (Manchester: Manchester University Press).

J.B. Jones & D. Balsom (eds) (2000), *The Road to the National Assembly for Wales* (Cardiff: University of Wales Press).

G. Jordan & L. Stevenson, 'Redemocratizing Scotland. Towards the Politics of Disappointment?', in A. Wright (ed) (2000), *Scotland: the Challenge of Devolution* (Aldershot: Ashgate).

M. Keating (2005), *The Government of Scotland* (Edinburgh: Edinburgh University Press).

M. Keating, L. Stevenson, P. Cairney & K. Taylor (2003), 'Does Devolution Make a Difference? Legislative Output and Policy Divergence in Scotland', *Journal of Legislative Studies*, 9, 3, pp. 110-39.

C. Kidner (2006), *Equal Opportunities: Scottish Executive Policy Overview* 2006 SPICe briefing 06/90 (See also the strand-specific briefings on Race Equality (06/84), Gender Identity and Sexual Orientation (06/85), Religion and Belief (06/86), Gender (06/87), Disability (06/88), and Age (06/89)) www.scottish.parliament.uk/business/research/index.htm.

T.C. Lundberg (2008), 'An Opposing View of Scotland's Ballot Paper Problem: Arbuthnott and the Government had the Right Idea', *The Political Quarterly*, Vol. 79, No. 4, pp. 569-77.

M. McAteer & M. Bennett (2005), 'Devolution and Local Government: Evidence from Scotland', *Local Government Studies*, 31(3): pp. 285-306.

A. McConnell (2004), *Scottish Local Government* (Edinburgh: Edinburgh University Press).

N. McGarvey & P. Cairney (2008), *Scottish Politics* (Basingstoke: Palgrave).

E. McLaughlin (2007), 'From Negative to Positive Equality Duties: The Development and Constitutionalisation of Equality Provisions in the UK', *Social Policy and Society,* Vol. 6.

B. McNair (2009), *News and Journalism In the UK*, 5th edition (London: Routledge).

J. Mitchell (2000), 'New Parliament, New Politics in Scotland', *Parliamentary Affairs*, Vol. 53, pp. 605–21.

T. Nairn (1997), *Faces of Nationalism* (London: Verso).

P. Norris (1995), 'Introduction: The Politics of Electoral Reform', *International Political Science Review*, Vol.16.

R. Parry (1999), 'Quangos and the Structure of the Scottish Public Sector', *Scottish Affairs*, 29, pp. 12-17.

L. Paterson, A. Brown, J. Curtice & K. Hinds (2001), *New Scotland, New Politics?* (Edinburgh: Edinburgh University Press).

R. Rawlings (2003), *Delineating Wales: Constitutional, Legal and Administrative Aspects of National Devolution* (Cardiff: University of Wales Press).

G. Reid (2006), *The fourth principle: the Stevenson Lecture on Citizenship, University of Glasgow 23 November 2006*, available at:
www.scottish.parliament.uk/corporate/po/george_reid_stevenson_lecture_2006.pdf.

K. Reif & H. Schmitt (1980), 'Nine Second-Order National Elections. A Conceptual Framework for the Analysis of European Election Results', *European Journal of Political Research*, 8, pp. 3-44.

J.J. Richardson & A.G. Jordan (1979), *Governing Under Pressure* (Oxford: Martin Robertson).

Scottish Executive (2001), *Public Bodies: Proposals for Change*
www.scotland.gov.uk/Publications/2001/06/9364/File-1.

Scottish Government and COSLA (2007), *Concordat between the Scottish Government and Local Government* available at
www.scotland.gov.uk/Resource/Doc/923/0054147.pdf.

Scottish Government, *Choosing Scotland's Future, A National Conversation*, at
www.scotland.gov.uk/Resource/Doc/194791/0052321.pdf.

Scottish Government (2008), *Simplifying Public Services* available at
www.scotland.gov.uk/Topics/Government/PublicServiceReform/simplifyingpublicservices.

Scottish Parliament Equal Opportunities Committee (2007), *Equalities in Scotland: A Review of Progress* (SP Paper 781) available at
www.scottish.parliament.uk/business/committees/equal/reports-07/eor07-03.htm.

Scottish Parliament Procedures Committee (2003), 3rd Report, *Report on the Founding Principles of the Scottish Parliament: The Application of Access and Participation, Equal Opportunities, Accountability and Power-sharing in the Work of the Parliament*, (SP Paper 818), available at www.scottish.parliament.uk/business/committees/historic/procedures/reports-03/prr03-03-01.htm.

Scottish Parliament Procedures Committee (2004), 6th Report, (Session 2), *A New Procedure for Members' Bills* (SP Paper 193).

Scottish Parliament Procedures Committee (2004), 7th Report, (Session 2), *Timescales and Stages of Bills* (SP Paper 228).

M. Shephard, N. McGarvey & M. Cavanagh (2001), 'New Scottish Parliament, New Scottish Parliamentarians?', *Journal of Legislative Studies*, 2, pp. 79-104.

Steel Commission (2006), *Moving to Federalism – A New Settlement for Scotland*, at www.scotlibdems.org.uk/files/steelcommission.pdf.

K. Strom, 'Parliamentary Committees in European Democracies', in L. D. Longley & R. H. Davidson (eds) (1998), *The New Roles of Parliamentary Committees* (London: Frank Cass).

R. Wyn Jones & R. Scully, 'Welsh Devolution: The end of the beginning, and the beginning of...?' in A. Trench (ed) (2008), The *State of the Nations 2008* (Exeter: Imprint Academic).

Biographies

Paul Cairney is Lecturer in Politics at the University of Aberdeen and editor of the *Scotland Devolution Monitoring Report*. His major research interests are in theories of public policy, public policy in the UK since devolution, Scottish politics (including the role of the Scottish Parliament, legislative change and Sewel motions), interest groups, and elites in Scotland and the UK.

Chris Carman is a Senior Research Lecturer in Policy Change and Civil Governance at the University of Strathclyde. He has previously taught at the University of Glasgow and the University of Pittsburgh.

John Curtice is Professor of Politics and Co-Director of the Centre for Elections and Representation Studies at the University of Strathclyde, and a Research Consultant to the Scottish Centre for Social Research. He is co-author of *Revolution or Evolution? The 2007 Scottish Elections* (Edinburgh University Press) and co-editor of *Has Devolution Worked?* (Manchester University Press).

Alex Fergusson MSP was elected as the Parliament's third Presiding Officer in May 2007. As Presiding Officer, in addition to chairing proceedings in the parliamentary chamber, he also chairs the Scottish Parliamentary Corporate Body, the Parliamentary Bureau and represents the Scottish Parliament at home and abroad. Before becoming an MSP in 1999, he spent 30 years farming sheep and cattle on his family farm in South Ayrshire.

Darren Halpin is Reader in Public Policy at Robert Gordon University, Aberdeen. His research focuses principally on interest groups and their involvement in the policy process. He is engaged in two Economic and Social Research Council (ESRC)-funded research projects, the UK Policy Agendas project and a study of group engagement in Scottish policy consultations. He was recently awarded a Leverhulme Research Fellowship to examine the organisational evolution of UK interests groups.

Chris Himsworth is Professor of Administrative Law at the University of Edinburgh. He has research interests which range across much of the public law field. Recent publications have focused on constitutional law in Scotland, administrative law (especially judicial review), and local government law. Another research interest is in environmental law in both its theoretical and more practical aspects.

Charlie Jeffery is Professor of Politics and Co-Director of the Institute of Governance at the University of Edinburgh. He directed the ESRC's programme on Devolution and Constitutional Change (2000-06). He is also a member of the Hansard Society Scotland Working Group.

Robert Johns is Lecturer in Politics at the University of Strathclyde. He was Principal Investigator on the Scottish Election Study 2007, and researches in the fields of electoral behaviour, public opinion and survey methodology.

James Johnston has been a clerk in the Scottish Parliament since 1999 and has recently completed a secondment to the House of Lords. Previously he completed a doctoral thesis on industrial decline and post-war Labour governments at the University of Birmingham. His published work includes a joint-authored book on post-war British politics.

Grant Jordan is Professor of Politics at the University of Aberdeen. He is currently working on an ESRC-supported project on population trends in UK interest group system.

Michael Keating is a political scientist specialising in nationalism, European politics and regional politics. He is Professor of Political and Social Sciences at the European University Institute in Florence, Italy, on secondment from the University of Aberdeen, where he holds the post of Professor of Politics.

Fiona Mackay is Senior Lecturer in Politics at the University of Edinburgh. She writes and researches on women and politics, gender and devolution (as part of the ESRC Devolution and Constitutional Change Programme 2000-06), and gender and equalities policy. She edited the *Gender Audit* (1996-2000) for the Scottish women's organisation, Engender; and she has been active in campaigns for women's representation in public and political life. She is also a member of the Hansard Society Scotland Working Group.

David McCrone is Professor of Sociology, and Co-Director of the University of Edinburgh's Institute of Governance. He is a Fellow of the Royal Society of Edinburgh, and a Fellow of the British Academy. He coordinated the research programmes funded by the Leverhulme Trust on Constitutional Change and National Identity (1999-2005), and on National Identity, Citizenship and Social Inclusion (2006-11).

Nicola McEwen is Senior Lecturer in Politics at the University of Edinburgh. She is an Associate Director of the Institute of Governance, and Co-Convenor of the PSA specialist group on British and Comparative Territorial Politics. She served on the Commission on Boundary Differences and Voting Systems (Arbuthnott Commission), established by the Secretary of State for Scotland in August 2004.

Neil McGarvey is Lecturer in Government at the University of Strathclyde. He has worked as consultant to the Scottish Local Government Information Unit, Department of Environment, Transport and the Regions, and Department for International Development.

Joyce McMillan chairs the Hansard Society Scotland Working Group and is a member of the Council of the Hansard Society. She writes a commentary column on political and social issues for *The Scotsman* newspaper, and she is also their chief theatre critic. She broadcasts regularly on BBC Radio Scotland and Radio Four and became a Visiting Professor of Queen Margaret University, Edinburgh in 2006. She was a member from 1998–99 of the British government's Consultative Steering Group on procedures for the new Scottish Parliament.

Brian McNair is Professor of Journalism and Communication at the University of Strathclyde. He is the author of several books and scholarly articles on the media and democracy, and is a regular contributor to the print, online and broadcast media in Scotland. His most recent book is *News & Journalism in the UK* (5th edition, Routledge 2009).

Emma Megaughin is the Projects Manager for Hansard Society Scotland. She is responsible for managing the production of Hansard Society educational resources for Scottish schools, and runs additional activities and projects that consider issues relating to the Scottish Parliament and the implications and lessons for other parts of UK parliamentary democracy. She also manages the Postgraduate Certificate in Governmnent & Public Policy, in association with the University of Edinburgh.

James Mitchell holds a chair in Politics at Strathclyde University. His research interests are in territorial politics: politics of regional government and devolution; national and regional identity; and the territorial aspects of public policy. His most recent book is *Devolution in the United Kingdom* (2009 Manchester University Press) and he is co-author of *Voting for a Scottish Government: The Scottish Parliament Election of 2007* (2010 MUP). He is currently completing a study of the SNP to be published by Oxford University Press. He is also a member of the Hansard Society Scotland Working Group.

Richard Parry is Reader in Social Policy in the School of Social and Political Science at the University of Edinburgh. His work falls in the interconnected areas of public policy, public administration and public sector resource allocation at Scottish, UK and European levels.

Lindsay Paterson is Professor of Educational Policy at the University of Edinburgh. He has written widely on Scottish politics, Scottish education, and the relationship of education to civic values. He has been an adviser to the Scottish Parliament's education committee.

Peter Riddell chairs the Hansard Society, is Chief Political Commentator of *The Times* and a Senior Fellow of the Institute for Government. He chaired the advisory board of the ESRC programme on devolution and constitutional change. He has written six books on British politics and is an Honorary Doctor of Literature at the University of Edinburgh.

Mark Shephard is Senior Lecturer in Politics at Strathclyde University. He is a member of the American Political Science Association, a member of the Study of Parliament Group and a member of the *Journal of Legislative Studies* editorial board. Current projects include research on the Scottish Parliament, Scottish campaign literature, and candidate image and the vote.

Lord Steel of Aikwood was an MP from 1965–97 and, from 1976–88 was leader of the Liberal Party. In 1997 he was knighted and elevated to the House of Lords before becoming, in 1999 the Scottish Parliament's first Presiding Officer, a position he held until the 2003 Scottish parliamentary elections.

Bill Thomson is an Assistant Clerk/Chief Executive at the Scottish Parliament. In addition to his corporate role, he has particular responsibility for the Public Affairs Group (which includes the teams delivering education and outreach, broadcasting, media relations, visitor services, external liaison, events and exhibitions and corporate publications) and for the newly established Research Information and Reporting Group. He joined the staff of the parliament in 1999 as Head of the Chamber Office, and subsequently held the posts of Head of Implementation (for migration to Holyrood), Director of Clerking and Reporting, then Director of Access and Information. He is a member of the Hansard Society Scotland Working Group.

Alan Trench is Research Fellow at the Europa Institute, University of Edinburgh and is Constitutional Adviser to Cymru Yfory/Tomorrow's Wales.

Luath Press Limited

committed to publishing well written books worth reading

LUATH PRESS takes its name from Robert Burns, whose little collie Luath (*Gael.*, swift or nimble) tripped up Jean Armour at a wedding and gave him the chance to speak to the woman who was to be his wife and the abiding love of his life. Burns called one of 'The Twa Dogs' Luath after Cuchullin's hunting dog in Ossian's *Fingal*. Luath Press was established in 1981 in the heart of Burns country, and is now based a few steps up the road from Burns' first lodgings on Edinburgh's Royal Mile.

Luath offers you distinctive writing with a hint of unexpected pleasures.

Most bookshops in the UK, the US, Canada, Australia, New Zealand and parts of Europe either carry our books in stock or can order them for you. To order direct from us, please send a £sterling cheque, postal order, international money order or your credit card details (number, address of cardholder and expiry date) to us at the address below. Please add post and packing as follows: UK – £1.00 per delivery address; overseas surface mail – £2.50 per delivery address; overseas airmail – £3.50 for the first book to each delivery address, plus £1.00 for each additional book by airmail to the same address. If your order is a gift, we will happily enclose your card or message at no extra charge.

Luath Press Limited
543/2 Castlehill
The Royal Mile
Edinburgh EH1 2ND
Scotland
Telephone: 0131 225 4326 (24 hours)
Fax: 0131 225 4324
email: sales@luath.co.uk
Website: www.luath.co.uk